SUPERSTITIONS

T0244209

A list of published works of this author by this press
appears at the end of this volume

Ahmad Kasravi
1890 - 1946

Ahmad Kasravi

SUPERSTITIONS

Translated from the Persian by
M. R. Ghanoonparvar

Mazda Publishers
2024

Publication of this book was made possible by a grant from
The A. K. Jabbari Trust

Mazda Publishers, Inc.
Academic publishers since 1980
P.O. Box 2603
Costa Mesa, California 92628 U.S.A.
www.mazdapublishers.com
A. K. Jabbari, Publisher

Copyright © 2024 by Mazda Publishers, Inc.
All rights reserved. No parts of this publication may be
reproduced or transmitted by any form or by any means without
written permission from the copyright holder except in the case of
brief quotations embodied in critical articles and reviews.

Library of Congress Control Number: 2024933987

ISBN 10: 1-56859-399-6
ISBN 13: 978-1-56859-399-9
Softcover (alk. paper)

Since this book is about families and relevant to women more than others, I dedicate it to the women of pure religion.
Ahmad Kasravi

CONTENTS

Foreword

Superstitions in Iran/Persia:
The Curious Quirks of *Shi'a* Belief

Superstitions have pervaded Iranian society for centuries, in particular after the advent of *Shi'a* Islam and more specifically since the rise and eventual fall of the Safavid Empire (1501–1736). These are defined as questionable, even irrational, beliefs often fostered by supposed communication with supernatural forces.

From such practices as *estekhareh*[1] to carrying lucky charms, superstitions manifest in various forms and offer a fascinating glimpse into the Iranian psyche. On the whole, these beliefs were encouraged by the actions and writings of the Shi'a clerics, popularly known as the *akhund*s, *mullah*s, or *ayatollah*s, and established mainly by their determination to find convenient means of control over illiterate people (and even those with formal education[2]). Thus, the people who followed the

---

[1] *Estekhareh* is a Shi'a Islamic practice of seeking guidance from Allah before making important decisions, particularly when one is uncertain about a choice or course of action. It involves performing a special prayer called *Salat al-Estekhareh.*

[2] It is indeed interesting to note the intersection of education and superstition in individuals. This example may serve to illustrate the point.

Mehdi Bazargan (1907–1995) was the first prime minister of the Islamic Republic of Iran. Educated in France, he became the head of the first engineering department at Tehran University in the late 1940s. During the oil nationalization period, he was appointed by Prime Minister Dr. Mohammad Mossadegh to be part of a team intending to take control of the Abadan oil refineries from the British. He writes in his mem-

desired rituals and prayers were provided a false sense of
security and comfort in an unpredictable world.

More examples of similar practices and beliefs
common in Iran are as follows:

> **1. The Evil Eye**: The belief in the evil
> eye, or *"nazar zadan,"* supposes that certain
> individuals have the power to cause harm or
> misfortune to others simply by looking at them
> with envy or malice. Protection against the
> evil eye may involve wearing amulets, reciting
> prayers, or performing rituals to ward off its
> effects.
>
> **2. Talismanic Objects**: Protective pow-
> ers are often thought to accompany certain tal-
> ismanic objects, such as amulets, charms, or
> written prayers. Talismans may keep one from
> harm or evil influences, though their use is not
> universally accepted within Islamic teachings.
>
> **3. Dream Interpretation**: Dream inter-
> pretation plays a significant role in many Is-
> lamic cultures, with certain dreams believed to
> hold prophetic or symbolic significance. Inter-
> pretations of dreams may vary widely depend-

---

oirs that before he could accept this critical position, he went
to see Ayatollah Mahmoud Talqani and asked him to perform
the e*stekhareh* ritual. Because the results were positive, he
therefore accepted the position.

Mehdi Bazargan's reliance on the *estekhareh* ritual before accepting a critical position showcases how personal beliefs can influence decision making, even in highly educated
individuals. This phenomenon is not uncommon and high-
lights the complexity of human psychology and belief sys-
tems.

Source: *Shast sal Khedamat va Moqavemat: Khaterat-e Mo-
handdes Mehdi Bazargan* [Bazargan Memories, Sixty-Years
of Service and Opposition. Introduced and edited by Col.
Gholamreza Nejati.] Tehran, Rasa Publications, 1375/1996, p.
276 (in Persian).

ing on cultural traditions and individual beliefs.

4. Taboos and Rituals: Various taboos
and rituals may be observed in different Islamic cultures, such as avoiding certain actions or behaviors during specific times or occasions believed to be unlucky.

Ahmad Kasravi has addressed these and many
other such absurd practices in this book. It is important
to note that while these superstitions may be prevalent
in many Islamic communities, they are not specific to
Islamic teachings. The other two Abrahamic religions
also abound with such superstitions. For example, the
burning bush, parting of the sea, walking on water, and
turning water to wine are examples advocated by their
respective clerics to control the people and discourage
rational thinking.

Volumes of literature have been compiled by the
Shi'a clerics throughout the centuries, a single one of
them enough to poison the mind and impair a person
from thinking rationally. One such notorious example is
Mohammad Baqer Majlesi's *Behar ol-Anwar*[3] [Oceans
of Light], a compilation of 102 volumes in the Arabic
language of predominantly Shi'a tradition and teachings,
the *hadith* which covers various aspects of Shi'a theol-
ogy, jurisprudence, ethics, and history. The book contains a vast array of traditions falsely attributed to the
Arab Prophet Mohammad, his family (*Ahl al-Bayt*), and
other prominent figures in Sh'ia Islam. The author later

---

[3] The *Behar ol-Anwar* is an immense Hadith compilation in
Arabic, running to 102 volumes. Mohammad Baqer Majlesi
also wrote more popular books in Persian, including biogra-
phies of the Arab Prophet Mohammad and the twelve
Imams. His persecution of Iranian Sonnites, Sufis, Jews, and
Zoroastrians was one of the causes of the weakening of the
Safavid monarchy.

wrote an abridged version in Persian called *Heliyyat –ol Mottaqin.*

There are many such books written mostly by the Iranian Shi'a clerics. Ali Dashti has eloquently said,

> Majlesi's *Behar ol-Anwar* is not excep-
> tional. It is not the only book which states
> that a fish named Karkara son of Sarsara son
> of Gharghara told Ali b. Abi Taleb where to
> ford the Euphrates before the battle of Sef-
> fin. Hundreds of books of this type are in
> circulation in Iran, for example *Helyat ol-
> Mottaqin, Jannat ol-Qolub, Anvar-e No`mani,
> Mersad ol-'Ebaid,* and many collections of sto-
> ries of prophets and *'olamai.* A single one
> of them is enough to poison a nation's mind
> and impair its capacity to think.[4]

Unfortunately, what we consider superstition per-
sists despite advancements in science and technology to
the contrary. In an age of rationality, one might assume
that superstitions would fade into obscurity. However,
they endure, fueled by clerics who encourage the long-
held but untenable power of blind belief in machinations
of the human psyche above that of logic. Even the most
logical minds can sometimes succumb to superstitions
under the right circumstances, revealing the deeply in-
grained nature of these irrational beliefs. Moreover, superstitions often arise in situations where individuals
lack control or understanding. In times of crisis or up-
heaval, superstitions offer a sense of urgency, however
illusory it may be.

In this volume, Ahmad Kasravi advocates for a ra-

---

[4] Ali Dashti, *Twenty-Three Years: A Study of the Prophetic
Career of Mohammad,* translated from the Persian by F. R. C.
Bagley. Costa Mesa, CA, Mazda Publishers, 1994 (10th print-
ing, 2021).

tional approach to understanding historical figures and events, free from embellishment and superstition. This perspective reflects a rationalist viewpoint that prioritizes empirical evidence and logical reasoning over religious or mystical interpretations of the world. It underscores the importance of promoting critical thinking and skepticism to counteract the influence of unfounded beliefs and superstitions.

A. K. Jabbari

Mr. A. K. Jabbari, the founder of Mazda Publishers, is a prominent figure in the world of Iranian studies. He holds B.S. and M.S. degrees in Aerospace Engineering from the Pennsylvania State University and a PhD in economics from Washington University in St. Louis, Mo. He was assistant professor of economics and management at Centre College of Kentucky from 1976 to 1979.

Mr. Jabbari has played a significant role in expanding the availability of scholarly works on Iran/Persia and has contributed to the field of Iranian studies through his publishing efforts. Mazda Publishers has published numerous books covering a wide range of topics, including Persian literature, history, art, philosophy, and linguistics. The publishing house has made valuable contributions to the dissemination of knowledge about Iranian culture and has been recognized as a reputable source for scholars, researchers, and enthusiasts interested in Iran and Persian studies.

Translator's Preface

Oxford Dictionary defines superstition as "the belief that particular events happen in a way that cannot be explained by reason or science; the belief that particular events bring good or bad luck." Similarly, Merriam Webster Dictionary describes superstition as "a belief or practice resulting from ignorance, fear of the unknown, trust in magic or chance, or a false conception of causation," "an irrational abject attitude of mind toward the supernatural, nature, or God resulting from superstition," and "a notion maintained despite evidence to the contrary." In this book, Ahmad Kasravi's definition of "Pendarha," his own neologism for the more common Persian term for superstitions, "khorafat," covers almost all aspects of the dictionary definitions cited above.

Arguably, one of the most prolific and controversial thinkers and writers of twentieth-century Iran, Ahmad Kasravi (1890-1946) is the author of numerous books and articles on all aspects of his society. His works cover a variety of subjects such as history, linguistics, geography, philology, literature, and religion, among others. As a reformist, his main campaign was against what he viewed as decadent ideas and superstitious beliefs in all aspects of the society.

Born in a religious family and the grandson of a clergyman, at an early age, Kasravi attended a seminary to become a cleric, which his late father had wished him to be. Although he did finish his studies at the seminary and began preaching, his liberal-minded sermons did not please the orthodox Shi'ite clerics and he soon became disillusioned with that profession and abandoned it.

While praising the Prophet of Islam and his religion, Kasravi's criticism of Islam as it is still practiced today, and of Shi'ism and the Shi'ite clergy in particular, to a great extent is in regard to the superstitious beliefs that they have inculcated in the people. As he was a former Shi'ite cleric, an insider who had turned traitor, as it were, many well-known Shi'ite clerics could no longer tolerate Kasravi's attacks on their beliefs, and issued religious decrees for his demise. He was stabbed with knives and assassinated by Feda'ian-e Islam (the Devotees of Islam), the followers of Navab-Safavi, a fanatical Shi'ite cleric, in the courthouse of Tehran in 1946.

This translation is based on Ahmad Kasravi, *Pendarha*, 2nd edition (Tehran: Peyman Printing House, 1945). The first edition was published in 1943.

The volume includes a select bibliography of Kasravi's work in addition to excerpts from an introductory article to my translation of Ahmad Kasravi's two books in one volume, *On Islam* and *Shi'ism*, published by Mazda Publishers in 1990.

In the Pure Name of the Creator

Foretelling, fortunetelling, geomancy, astrology, palm reading, face reading, witchcraft, enchantment, magic, prayer charms, exorcism, channeling the dead, good and bad omens, and the like are all harmful practices that deviate from the laws of nature, and since they stem from superstitious beliefs, we have discussed all of them under the heading of "superstitions." Since, however, in terms of their nature they belong to several categories, we have separated them and will discuss them one by one.

Kasravi

زعفر جنی با سپاه خود (در میدان کربلا)

Za'far Jenni. In popular Shi'ite belief, Za'far Jenni was the king of the Jinn, who came with his army to assist Imam Hoseyn in his battle against his enemies. Hoseyn, however, did not allow him since he said it was unfair for the Jinn who could see the humans to fight the humans to whom the Jinn were invisible.

Chapter One

Is Foretelling Possible?

Is foretelling possible? Is it possible to know about future events or the unseen? Do human beings have such power? Does such power exist in the external world?

Other than "no," no answer can be given to such questions. We cannot know about future events and the unseen. Humans do not have such power, and such solutions cannot be found in the external world.

Among people, however, such practices prevail, and we shall discuss them separately.

1. Foretelling

The wish to know about the future and what will happen is inherent in everyone's nature. When a major event (such as the present war[1]) occurs, everyone seeks its end and wishes to know how it will end.

However, as I stated before, neither do humans have such a power nor is there an instrument for such in the external world. It is impossible for anyone to know about the future or about the unseen.

Yes, by observing certain things, one can determine the outcome. For instance, by observing the condition of a patient, a physician can sometimes conclude whether the patient will recover or die. When a war occurs between two governments, if a person is aware of the power of each government, the resolve of its masses, and the like, he can easily ascertain the outcome of the war

---

[1] World War II.

and which side will be the victor and which side will be defeated. We always determine next year's abundance or shortage of food from whether there is heavy or no rainfall.

Such things can be determined, but this is forecasting, not foretelling. We must distinguish between foretelling and forecasting. I repeat: Foretelling is impossible. Those who engage in foretelling do so because they suffer from psychological incapacity. And occasionally, there are charlatans who profit from such practices, who deceive the people and rob them of their money. Up to four years ago, in Tehran, I used to see a person by the name of Safa who would visit people's homes and obtain money from them by foretelling.

One day he came to me. Since he was talking a great deal about the future, I told him: "If you tell me about the past and I find it to be the truth, I will also believe what you tell me about the future."

He said: "You are from the lineage of a king."

I said: "Our family has consisted of Seyyeds, descendants of the Prophet."

He said: "Your lineage to that king is through your mother."

I asked: "What was his name? When did he rule?"

He could not answer, and since he found me to be aloof, he got up and left.

Some people imagine that if a person lives an ascetic life of hardship, he will acquire the power to know about the future and the unseen. This, however, is a superstitious belief. We know of no one who has acquired such power by living a life of hardship, and all we hear about such things is boasting.

Some Sufi pivot would say that he knew the future, but he would not provide any proof regarding the veracity of his claim. During our own time, there are many such pivots and many ascetics. Test them. Can they tell us about the world ten years hence?

Some people mention Indian yogis as an example and say that yogis endure exhausting hardship; for instance, one of them stands on one foot for years, another hangs on a tree with one hand for several years, and as a result of suffering such hardship, they acquire the power of knowing about the future and the unseen, and also know everyone's secrets.

My response is: Yogis live far away from us, and we do not know anything about them. What we hear about what they do is all hearsay, which cannot be believed. In such cases, people lie a lot and also deceive themselves. People who would not lie in other instances would not avoid lying in such cases. This is something that we have tested many times.

On the other hand, we see that if the yogis were capable of knowing about the unseen or the future, people could greatly benefit from them. Masses of people would assemble at their doors, thousands of people would surround them, and they would benefit from their foretelling.

Others such as governments could benefit greatly from them. The British government that controls the country of the yogis could ask them about other countries and learn about their secrets.

In the current war which has been going on for several years between England, Russia, and the United States against Germany, Italy, and Japan, we saw that in the second year of the war, Japan, which until that time was neutral, suddenly started to fight and invaded Malaysia and other countries under the rule of the British and the United States and made significant advancements. The British suffered defeats one after another and this was difficult for them. They put pressure on Mr. Churchill, the British prime minister, in the Parliament to the extent that his Cabinet was about to fall. Mr. Churchill said that the possibility of Japan entering the war had been low and that is why he had not properly prepared mobilization against it.

Here we might ask, why didn't Mr. Churchill want to make use of the talent of Indian yogis to learn about the intention of Japan and not be taken by surprise? Was Churchill negligent, or is it that the story of yogis' knowledge of the unseen is a lie? Which one of these two choices is acceptable?

Today, every government wishes to know the secrets of other governments, and as we know, they send spies to learn about those secrets and waste a great deal of money. I ask: If the story about yogis is true, why waste so much money and energy? Why does every government not hire one or a few of those yogis and benefit from their knowledge? Why does the British government not employ the yogis for its Intelligence Service?

We have heard that many yogis engage in panhandling. They attract the attention of the people with their astonishing acts and demand money from them. This itself is an indication of their abjectness. How abject should a group be in a place such as India to be incapable of making a living and to have to extend their hands to this or that person for help? Should this be the result of suffering hardship?

Then, this itself is a problem, when certain people who know about the unseen and are aware of their own future would not benefit from this knowledge in order to become needless of panhandling. If a yogi knows about the future and the unseen, why would he not find a treasure among the hidden treasures buried in the earth and by digging it out, become rich and needless? Why not make a great deal of money from the people by showing them the thieves and the place of what they have stolen? Why not engage in business and trade and gain huge profits by foretelling the increase in the price of certain goods?

At this point, we must say that a tree is known for its fruit. Let a yogi suffer as much hardship as he wants to and do whatever he wants to do. Just because in the end he engages in panhandling is indisputable proof that what he does is baseless and futile.

As I said, foretelling is a human desire, or rather, a human mental illness. Frequently, certain individuals claim the ability of foretelling and spread the practice among the people; but thus far, every foretelling has turned out to be false.

You cannot point to one foretelling that has turned out to be true. This itself is proof that such a thing is impossible. In every foretelling, people grab one little point that has turned out to be true and close their eyes to all the other parts. Here, I will give you an example.

In 1914 when World War I began, European newspapers published a prediction by the famous Russian philosopher, Tolstoy, which was also translated and published in Persian newspapers, and everywhere they placed a great deal of value on it. Here I quote a summary of what was published in *Asr-e Jadid* newspaper:

"In 1913, Europe will be in great flames and it will begin with the countries in southeast Europe. This conflagration will gradually increase and spread to all Europe in 1914. In that year, I see all of Europe in flames and bleeding. I hear the lamentations of huge bloody battlefields. But about the year 1915, a strange figure from the north—a new Napoleon—enters the stage of the bloody drama. He is a man of little militaristic training, a writer or a journalist, but in his grip most of Europe will remain till 1925. The end of the great calamity will mark a new political era for the old world. There will be left no empires and kingdoms, but the world will form a federation of the United States of Nations."

The Sphere magazine published in London had published this piece and added: "This entire prediction was

presented to His Imperial Majesty, the Emperor of Russia, and from there it was sent to the Emperor of Germany, who was quite astonished."

They published this prediction in newspapers and
monthly magazines and said that it had turned out to be
true, because the war started in 1914, as Tolstoy had
predicted. However, if you think about it carefully, you
will find that all turned out to be false.

He had predicted the start of the war to be 1913,
whereas it began in 1914. The journalists were so overjoyed that they disregarded the difference of one year.

Who was that "strange figure" who was supposed to
come from the north in 1915 and had in his grip most of
Europe? And why did he not come? At the end of the
war, he had predicted a new political era for the world,
which had all turned out to be false.

This is one example of prediction and how false it
turns out to be. It is astonishing for a person such as Tolstoy to engage in such practice.

How could he have made such predictions? If it was
forecasting, that is not how it should be, and if it was
foretelling, how and with what kind of power did he
know it?

At this point, I must say that human wishful thinking has no bounds. A man who worked so hard to become Tolstoy also was afflicted with such wishful thinking at that time, and he also could find certain people to
toy with at the time.

This illness escalates during wartime and afflicts
scholars and famous people more than everyone else.

The current war that began five years ago among
great nations has also resulted in many predictions which
have been published in newspapers. All of them have
turned out to be hollow and baseless. It is regrettable that
people still place value on foretelling and yet again are
deceived by charlatans.

Last year, one of the Persian newspapers published an article under the heading, "A Celestial Foretelling," in which it stated that Safi Ali Shah in his interpretation of the Koran, which is in verse, has made a prediction regarding the Koranic verse "Allah effaces what He will"[2] as follows:

> In the turning of time that we shall see
> In the year of thirteen sixty-three
> The time of the world will end herein
> And a brand new era will begin

The newspaper wrote: "These verses foretell that in 1363 [of the Islamic lunar calendar, approximately equivalent to 1943-1944 in the Gregorian calendar], which is two years hence, a new era will begin in the world."

I say, these two couplets do not have a clear meaning. The Persian and Arabic mixture "sisad-o shast-o seh alf" as he states it could mean either 363,000 or 1363. He then says, "And a brand new era will begin," but he does not say what that era will be or what changes will occur in the world and how. He needs to state all that to make any sense.

Moreover, how did Safi Ali Shah acquire such knowledge? If it is a verse from the Koran, how could it be interpreted in that way? Is the Koran a riddle that one person understands and another does not? If he has stated it on his own, what does it have to do with the Koran? And then, how did he know it?

It is astonishing that the person who brought forth God's message as the Koran [the Prophet Mohammad] was weary of knowledge of the unseen. He said: "I do not know the unseen." By means of the same Koran, Safi

---

[2] Koran, "The Thunder," Verse 39.

Ali Shah become the knower of the unseen and the future.

After all this, Safi Ali Shah says that "the time of the world will end," not about the end of the war and peace between governments. In the year 1363, which will be soon, I cannot surmise any event which could bring about the end of the world. Suppose Germany is defeated and the war ends. That would not be the end of the world and the beginning of a new era.

This prediction by Safi Ali Shah can only mean one thing. It conveys that its author fabricates falsehoods and engages in deception.

In the same Persian newspaper, other predictions by some Egyptian foretellers are published. One of them predicted that the war of Germany against England and Russia will end in 1942, but reconciliation and signing of treaties will be in 1943.

In Egypt, there have been certain soothsayers for many years who make a living in this way. One of them also published a monthly magazine in this connection.

The writer of the article in the Persian newspaper has also assumed that the above prediction was true, and reasons that that soothsayer had previously warned about the German war against Russia, which turned out to be true, since those two countries went to war.

I ask, if predictions are possible and these individuals are soothsayers, why do they not predict the whole thing at once? Why do they do it piece by piece? Why has that Egyptian not predicted all the events of the war and its outcome? Why has he told about the end of the war, but not about which side will win?

The truth is that a few charlatans have come forth, and since they have figured out certain things from the actions and speeches of politicians about the future, they state them as predictions. The field is very limited for their predictions, and that is why this year they only predict about next year, and next year about the following year. If it turns out to be true, it turns out to be true, and if it does not, it does not.

This is the way of the people. If a soothsayer or a fortuneteller tells a hundred lies, the people pay no attention and disregard them, but if one prediction turns out to be true, they grab that one as proof of his veracity.

The same is true regarding the Egyptian soothsayers. They have frequently said things that have turned out to be false without the people having paid attention. But when one of their statements turns out to be true, they use that one instance as proof and flaunt it before the people.

Many people knew about the possibility of the German war against Russia ahead of time. This is a general rule in politics in order not to allow the enemy to aggrandize. Germany and Russia are inevitable enemies. The aggrandizement of one would be the source of the destruction of the other. Hence, it would be incredible for the Russians to sit by silently and allow Germany to tolerate the British controlling the hand of Europe, to control all of Europe, to become a powerful government, and then invade Russian territory and disassemble the threads of that government. I personally have said frequently: "One of the astonishing things would be for Russia to stand aside in this war. There must be some secret that we do not know about, otherwise for that government to sit by silently would be a deviation of the policy of governments." My acquaintances had frequently heard me say this. It was not a prediction but rather a statement based on my knowledge.

In any case, the prediction of that Egyptian also turned out to be false, and right now as I write these lines, it is the end of 1942, and there is not the slightest sign of the ending of the war. The leaders of the governments of Russia, England, and the United States had a meeting last week in Tehran and engaged in consultation and talking about what strategies they should devise to be able to defeat Germany as soon as possible. This is another example that anyone who engages in soothsaying would reap no benefits, but rather, disgrace.[3]

Another point that needs to be mentioned is that since charlatans claim to be devout and pious, and on the other hand use soothsaying, knowledge of the unseen, and such practices as instruments for charlatanism, a false belief has spread among the people who believe a devout and pious person should know the unseen, be capable of knowing the future, and have the ability to accomplish astonishing feats of which others are incapable.

---

[3] Last August, one evening, BBC Persian told an elaborate story about one of the lamas (religious leaders in China, Burma, and Tibet) who got on a train. When the conductor came, he paid for his own ticket and that of the woman sitting next to him. Being a stranger, the woman protested as to why he had paid for her ticket. He answered: "Because your purse was stolen and you have no money." Upon hearing this, the woman started searching around her and realized that she did not have her purse. Astonished by this, the people started to ask the lama about the future and the past, such as when the war was going to end. The lama said that it would end on 25 October.
The announcer on London BBC Persian radio, who was telling this story enthusiastically, said: "25 October is 2 Aban." During those days, the Germans were hastily retreating in the east and west, and it was highly assumed that within a couple of months, they would be defeated and the war would end. That is why I thought that if this happened and the war ended a few days before or after 25 October, the lovers of superstitions would totally forget the predictions that had turned out to be false and would only flaunt this one before us. This made me uncomfortable, but we saw that October came and passed, the Persian year 1323 [1944] also ended, and still the war has not over.
(This note was added for the second printing of this book.)
This note is by Kasravi.

This is a false belief that has been widespread among the people for a long time, and many of the Sufi leaders and others have been deceived by this false belief, and in order to display their status to the people, they have engaged in soothsaying and claim to have knowledge of the unseen. Even if one of them has not engaged in such practices, his followers and supporters have later fabricated stories about him and recorded them in books. It is considered beneath the status of a Sufi elder or religious leader to not have knowledge of the unseen.

Those verses by Safi Ali Shah were for this purpose, but regarding Tolstoy, I have no idea as to whether he was deceived by this false belief or such desires had nested in his heart due to reclusiveness and old age.

Whatever the case may be, religious devotion and piety would not only not give anyone knowledge of the unseen. Religious devotion and piety in their true sense are for avoiding such practices. If a person is religious, he must know that God has not granted humans any power for knowing the unseen, and claiming to know about the unseen and engaging in soothsaying in addition to deceiving the people is also fighting God.

One of the great benefits that we seek from religion is for the people to learn the Divine rules of the universe, and to know the path that God has opened for living, for people to follow those rules and that path. This itself is a great foundation of religion.

Let me state it more clearly: The purpose of religion is to prevent certain people from desiring to be soothsayers, magicians, and the like, which are baseless and futile practices, and to not turn themselves and others away from the true path of life. It is utmost ignorance to imagine that certain people would achieve the knowledge of the unseen through religious devotion and piety.

Rather, if you assess carefully, you will find that most of those who engage in soothsaying and such practices are irreligious charlatans and hypocrites, and since they do not want to pursue a profession or occupation to make a legitimate living, they engage in such deceptive acts without fear of their many harmful consequences.

Soothsaying, for instance, in addition to being disobedience to God and Divine rules as well as fabricating lies, often can result in great harms. Right now as I am writing these lines, I have a book open before me which tells the story of the filicide of Mehmed III, the sultan of the Ottoman Empire. That sultan had a son by the name of Prince Mahmud, who was an honorable and competent young man. A deceptive hypocritical religious sheikh, or seer, gained access to the Prince through people who served his mother. The sheikh engaged in soothsaying and sent a message to the Prince stating that he would soon become the king. He also sent him some magic charms. Sultan Mehmed learned about this and discovered the things that the sheikh had sent. He was so enraged that he ordered to have Prince Mahmud arrested and strangulated. Then they also arrested his mother and supporters and tossed them into the sea. They also did the same thing to the deceptive sheikh. Because of the sorrow and distress of this foolish action, Sultan Mehmed also died within a month.[4]

Ottoman history is filled with many such occurrences. The same book contains a story about a dervish who had predicted: "A man whose name is the name of a bird will soon appear and become king." This wishful lie resulted in certain people thinking that they would become kings and engaging in certain efforts to achieve it. One person whose name was Shahin [royal falcon] made such an effort, and another whose name was Tayyar

---

[4] Although by and large, Kasravi's account of the story is accurate, certain details, including the date of the death of Sultan Mehmet, must have been recorded inaccurately in the book Kasravi had been reading. [Translator's note]

[flier] rose to the occasion, and both resulted in much bloodshed without accomplishing anything.

2. Fortunetelling

Fortunetelling is a part of soothsaying. There are two types of soothsaying. One type is without instruments (which I have already discussed) and another, with instruments, an example of which is fortunetelling. Fortunetellers want to say that they can have paths into the unseen and they can tell about the future.

Regarding the roots of fortunetelling and its history, this is what we have found. In ancient times, people worshipped idols. Every group of people imagined a few gods for themselves and had constructed temples and guardians for them. In history, we learn that these guardians were known as "*kohen*s" who claimed to be in communication with the gods and would act as intermediaries between the people and the gods, would receive answers to questions people had of the gods, and would foretell the future in the words of the gods.

One point worthy of note is that the people did not regard those gods or idols as much higher than humans. Rather, they regarded them as human-like beings with desires, grudges, envy, and such characteristics, beings who were deemed to have wives and children. Thus they turned to the gods regarding every event, sought their counsel, and asked about the outcome of some forthcoming affair. The catch, however, was that they would have to make a sacrifice for that god and bring a gift for the *kohen* in order to receive the answer.

Moreover, we also know about the gods' types of answers, consisting of vague statements which rarely proved to be false. For example, we know about Croesus who wanted to go to war against the Achaemenid king [Cyrus the Great]. He consulted the oracle of Delphi. The oracle received an answer from his god as follows: "If you go to war, you shall destroy a great empire."

From this statement, Croesus inferred that he would destroy the Achaemenid Empire. With much hope and confidence, he waged war, but he was defeated and his entire country fell to the Achaemenid king. Then people said: "What the god willed was the destruction of Croesus' kingdom. That god wanted to prevent him from going to war, but he did not understand the god's will."

This is a sample of the gods' responses. Indeed, fortunetelling began then, and as you can see, initially it was known as asking the gods certain questions through the *kohen*s, who brought back verbal responses. Later on, other ways were devised in which the gods would communicate their will in various ways. For instance, when sacrifices were made, the *kohen*s would learn about the gods' wrath or delight by reading the intestines of the sacrificed animal. They used to keep certain birds in the names of the gods, inferring some things from the birds' feeding or not feeding, and interpret their every movement. There were many such ways for figuring out whether the gods were wrathful or delighted, and for predicting the future.

Later still, there was no longer any need for the *kohen*s. Everyone would predict his own future and learn about his own and other people's fate from the flying of birds, the sounds of animals, the jumping up and down of four-legged beasts, the blowing of the winds, the cumulating of clouds, the re-blossoming of trees, the twitching of human skin, nightmares a person has every night, the appearance of comets, and hundreds of other ways. All these are varieties of fortunetelling. In Persian, they are called "marva" [good omen] and "morghova" [bad omen], which I will discuss separately.

During our time, there are other special ways for fortunetelling, which apparently did not exist in ancient times. These ways are varied and countless. Some people tell fortunes by using books. Others use other ways. For instance, at the beginning of the book, they have

"Abjad" letters [the Arabic numerical alphabet] in chessboard-shaped squares. The one asking for his fortune must close his eyes and place a finger on one of the squares. Each square has a description in the book. The fortuneteller reads the description out loud. This is the simplest of fortunetelling methods.

Old women tell fortunes with chickpeas. They arrange the chickpeas in certain shapes and interpret them. Fortunetelling by playing cards is a common practice among Europeans.

Fifty years ago, there existed a rock in a chamber in Qatlgah Cemetery in Mashhad. It was believed that any person who could lift that rock was not a "bastard." Many people assessed the purity of their ancestry by lifting that rock.

A few years ago, I saw a young man in Yazd, who had a bird in a cage with which he told fortunes. He had a stack of small pieces of paper on each of which he had written a sentence, such as, "it will end well," "you shall take a trip," "you will be regretful," or "you are the victim of black magic." He had the stack of papers fitted in the cage. When someone seeking to know his fortune would come to him, he would charge a certain amount of money, and by gesturing with his hand or head, signal to the bird, which would pick one of the pieces of paper and give it to the fortuneteller, who would unfold and read it. Since this was a new method of fortunetelling, it was in great demand, and people told many stories about the veracity of that fortuneteller.

It should be pointed out that the skill of these fortunetellers is revealed in the statements they choose. For instance:

"There is a mark on your body." Is there anyone who does not have some mark on his body, such as a mole, a healed wound, or pockmark?

"You wish people well, but people wish you ill." This is what most people believe about themselves.

"You wish to travel." Is there anyone who does not wish to travel?

"When you were fourteen years old, you dodged a danger due to the conjunction of two stars." What is a danger due to the conjunction of two stars, and how did the person dodge that danger? Everyone can think of some incident in his life.

"The Prophet Daniel says that you shall achieve great status." Is there anyone who would dislike such good tidings? And who would doubt the truthfulness of the Prophet Daniel?

"You have an enemy among your relatives." Is there anyone who does not have an enemy among his relatives?

I should say that, on the whole, from the oracle of the Delphi idol temple to the fortunetellers who roam the alleyways of Tehran, they have all studied in the same school, in that their deeds and words are similar. As I said, all these practices are falsehood and are baseless. No one knows about the unseen in the world, and no one can tell the future. All these methods are meaningless. After all, for what reason is a person who is unable to lift up a rock the offspring of adultery? What relationship is there between not being able to lift a rock and the immorality of one's lineage? Could there be any lie more shameless than this? Lifting or not lifting up a rock is indicative of the ability or inability of that person. What does it have to do with what his parents did or did not do?

How could the arrangement of chickpeas in a certain order be proof of someone going on a trip? Do chickpeas have intelligence? Are chickpeas knowledgeable about anyone's past and future and do they arrange themselves however they see fit? Could any superstition be more foolish than this?

What reason could possibly exist regarding the veracity of the fortunetelling book that they have fabricated to state that when a person closes his eyes and puts a finger on a certain letter, the statements written regarding that letter reveal that person's destiny? As though God has created that book and sent it for fortunetelling?

Such beliefs mean the attribution of falsehoods to God and are considered the greatest of sins. Moreover, the purpose of such practices is to deceive the people and discourage them from engaging in constructive work. This world operates on the basis of solid principles which everyone must understand and follow. Fortunetellers misguide the people and cause them to deviate from the laws of nature. These fortunetellers attribute falsehoods to God and wage battle against God.

People are unaware that hundreds of chaotic situations result from fortunetelling. Some fellow tells a woman: "A tall woman with black eyes and eyebrows is your enemy and has used black magic against you." That simpleminded woman believes this and begins to assume that her mother-in-law, the sister of her husband, the wife of her brother-in-law, or her cowife is her enemy, and hence she too engages in using black magic against that person. This has happened thousands of times.

Twenty years ago, when I was in Tabriz, the home of one of our relatives was robbed and they lost a huge amount of money. A fortuneteller told them: "A close, tall relative has committed this robbery." From what the fortuneteller said, our relative became suspicious of one of his wife's brothers. As this rumor spread little by little, the Police Department became suspicious of that brother and arrested and imprisoned him. A month later, the money was found elsewhere and it became known that the brother of his wife was innocent. This caused grave hostility between the husband and wife from which they suffered for many years.

There are hundreds, or rather thousands, of such stories. And still, such are the minor harmful consequences.

Some fortunetellers use fortunetelling as a tool for deceiving women and making them lose interest in their husbands by engaging in heinous acts. Some of them become an intermediary between women and male strangers. One of the things they do is to lure a woman into witchcraft and tell her: "You must commit a sin." And by saying this, they force chaste women to do unchaste things.

Sometimes, they lure women to deserts "to bury black magic charms" and hand them over to monstrous men in the desert. Such acts are among the masterworks of fortunetellers.

There are case files of such fortunetellers in the Tehran Prosecutor's Office, which I do not consider allowable to write about here.

3. Astrology

Astrology also engages in foretelling. As I said before, foretelling is sometimes simple and without tools and sometimes with tools. Astrology is a part of foretelling with tools.

Firstly, we should know that astrology is different from astronomy. Astronomy involves understanding the sun, the moon, the stars, and other luminaries in the sky, and is one of the most valuable sciences. Astrology, on the other hand, is for foretelling the future under the pretext of studying the sun, the moon, and the stars, which is all superstition and supposition.

Some interpret the revolving of the luminaries in the sky and their proximity to one another the basis on which they foretell the future. They assume that the events in the world and what occurs on earth stems from the revolving of the sun, the moon, and the stars in the sky and their positions. Hence, they figure out "the effect from the cause," and by observing the position of the stars (or as they say, the position of the planets), they determine future events and alert others.

They also point to certain hours and state that when certain things are done during those hours, since the stars are in such and such position, those things will or will not be achieved.

Obviously, such practices first appeared in ancient times and are mementos of the eras of idol worshipping. It is also obvious that such foretelling first began with comets and shooting stars (meteors) and certain features in the sky that are occasionally seen.

Since comets appear once every thirty to forty years, and every person sees them once or twice in his lifetime, whenever they appear, people become frightened and discuss them a great deal. This is still true in our own time.

In ancient times, the people considered it a sign of the wrath of the gods, and the *kohen*s would take advantage of the opportunity, predicting the coming of calamities such as cholera, plague, floods, or draught, thereby intensifying people's fears. They also displayed the same behavior when stars collapsed and certain signs such as redness or brightness appeared in the sky.

This opened the way for certain individuals to make use of the luminaries in the sky as a tool for soothsaying. They fabricated interpretations of the motions of the sun, the moon, and five other stars (which they called the seven revolving stars) which changed their position in the sky every day—or more accurately, among the other stars—occasionally becoming closer to one another and on other occasions, distanced from one another, thereby considering each motion a sign, or rather the cause of an event on Earth. The reason for the widespread belief in this superstition is that since in the simple life at that time, the people looked at the sky more often than in our time, and given that they did not have clocks, compasses, and other such instruments, they were more in need of understanding the stars and their motions. Moreover, large masses of the people at the time considered the revolving stars as gods, which they worshipped.

Whether as a result of the ancient people's beliefs regarding the revolving stars which they considered as gods or since they did not understand the operation of the world and the causes of events, the belief that the revolving of the sun, the moon, and the stars were the causes of events became a thriving market among the people, and escalated the popularity of astrology.

On the other hand, since understanding of the luminaries in the sky, their position in the sky, and their distance from or proximity to one another was not so simple for everyone, this part of soothsaying seemed scientific, and its practitioners were considered an elite group who gained status among the people.

No other superstitious belief (with the exception of communicating with the dead, which I will discuss later) became so organized and gained such value.

Another thing that in addition to the above increased the popularity of astrology and the deception of the people is that astrology has always been coupled with astronomy.

As I mentioned, astronomy is a valuable science with a solid foundation. This science was also known in ancient times, and from those times famous scientists were engaged in it. Although in most instances, they made mistakes, in certain instances they were successful. For example, they calculated the revolution of the stars correctly and they learned the position of each. That is why we see that since three thousand years ago, these scientists knew about the lunar and solar eclipses and predicted them ahead of time.

Lunar and solar eclipses and predicting them is based on calculations and are among the topics of astronomy. Based on calculation, an astronomer can tell us that on such and such a day at such and such an hour and such and such a minute, the sun, the moon, and the earth shall be in a certain position, the sun and the moon would be facing each other, and the earth would be in between, and the shadow of the earth would be cast on the moon and darken it. This can be known based on calculations and predicted ahead of its occurrence.

This is one of the tasks of science. However, because people do not know it, they think that an astronomer knows about the unknown, and they do not distinguish between this and other predictions which are superstitions, regarding them as true.

Still, in our own time, common people say: "If the astrologer does not know certain things, then why is it that when he predicts a lunar or solar eclipse it turns out to be true?" This has been the cause of people being deceived from ancient times. Also, the emergence of a new moon, when the moon is visible or unseen, the start of the new year, and matters of this sort, which are based on calculations, are proof for people to believe that the astrologers have knowledge of the unknown.

Thus it was that astrology was created and became known, and since in the second and third centuries after the advent of Islam [9th and 10th centuries CE], Greek philosophy and other Greek and Roman sciences spread to the East and became extremely common, astrology was also among those sciences. Based on what we know, from then on for a thousand years, astrology was so widespread that in addition to the common people, kings and rulers also believed in it, and every king had one or several astrologers in his court. If a king wanted to mount the throne, go to war, have a palace built, take on a wife, or any other major undertaking, the astrologer would have to choose an auspicious hour. During that period, astrologers had replaced the Delphi oracle. We find many astonishing stories in history, some of which I will recount here as proof:

Safavid kings had tremendous faith in astrologers and retained them in their royal courts. An astonishing

event occurred during the time of Shah Abbas I. Astrologers predicted: "The position of the stars indicate
that in this year, a king will be eliminated." Moreover,
regarding Shah Abbas, they said: "The ominous quadrature is positioned in the ascending square and the star of
fortune is in the abyss of decline and trouble." From
these two statements, they concluded that Shah Abbas
was in danger of some harm or mishap.

Since they did not surmise falsehood in what they
said, one of the astrologers, Mullah Jalal Yazdi, suggested that Shah Abbas must dethrone himself for three
days and abdicate the crown and the throne in favor of a
prisoner condemned to death, while during those three
days, all the ministers, military men, and others would
be under the command of that prisoner, and after three
days, he would be killed and in this way the Shah would
divert the calamity away from himself.

Fearing for his life, Shah Abbas had become obedi-
ent to the astrologers and he agreed to that suggestion.
Since several dervishes had been arrested during that
year on the charge of irreligiosity, they decided to make
a man by the name of Mullah Yusefi king and then have
him killed.

In *Alamara-ye Abbasi*, a history of the Safaid Dynasty, this story is recounted as follows:

They brought the abovementioned Yusefi to the
camp. His Highness deposed himself from the monarchy
and kingship and granted kingship unto that condemned
man and placed the crown of kingship upon his head and
dressed him in costly garb, and on the day of departure,
mounted him on a steed from the village of Barda' with
a bejeweled saddle and bridle and declared him king,
and all the commanders and courtiers and those who
served in the army and troops became his retinue in accordance with the protocols, accompanying him to the
Royal Palace. They served him a banquet of food and
drink, and at night the grand guards and victorious mili-

tary men stood watch. That poor man realized what was in store for him, thus he spent those three days in leisure. ... His Highness spent those three days riding with two or three vanguards and servants and did not attend to the affairs of the monarchy at all. While riding, Mullah Yusefi saw His Excellency Mullah Jalal, the astrologer, and asked him, 'Your Excellency, why have you set out to spill my blood?' ... In short, after three days, he was stripped of his borrowed garb of life and fell from the throne. After the abovementioned incident, His Highness once again mounted the seat of command.

The second story is also about one of the Safavid kings, Shah Abbas II. When Shah Abbas II died in 1666, they chose his son Safi Mirza as his successor. The astrologers chose the hour for his coronation and the young king sat on the throne.

In the first and second years of his reign, however, many disturbances occurred. On the one hand, Turkomans and Uzbeks engaged in raids and plunder, causing great harm, and on the other, a severe earthquake occurred in Shirvan and thereabouts and caused great damage. The people were displeased and unhappy with the king.

Moreover, the young king was weak, and since he associated and traveled around with women and did not see any boundaries in drinking and pleasures of the flesh, he became less healthy and more incapable day by day.

The court physician made a great deal of effort and tried every remedy, but given the excessive indulgence of the king, the physician's efforts were thwarted. On the other hand, the mother of the king, instead of persuading her son to practice abstinence, blamed the physician and called him ignorant. Since in an autocratic court, the result of this would be the killing of the physician and the confiscation of his wealth, he was tremendously afraid. That is why, in order to save his life and wealth, he spread the rumor that the court astrologer had made an error in choosing the hour for the coronation of the king, and that the ill health of the king, the lack of security in the country, the earthquake, and other such turmoil were all due to the inauspicious hour of the coronation.

Once these words became widespread, the courtiers unwisely believed it. The French traveler, Jean Chardin, who was in Iran at the time, writes about this story in his travel memoir as follows:

The king and his mother believed this nonsense more than anyone else. His Majesty's wives also had no doubt about the astrologer's fault. The court eunuchs and other sycophantic courtiers, who have no opinion other than the king's, followed the same belief. Hence, the physician advanced his scheme and in this way saved his own life, wealth, and reputation. No matter how the astrologer tried to prove his innocence, it was of no use. It reached a point when, fearing for his own life, he chose not only to keep silent, but also was compelled to confess to his own ignorance. Now they needed to make up for the past mistake. In order to do so, after a great deal of contemplation, they found no other way but for the king to have another coronation. Since the people did not regard the name "Safi" as a good omen and said that during the reign of Shah Safi I turmoil also occurred in Iran, as a result, they decided to once again choose another hour and coronate the king with another name. Hence, the astrologers worked hard to choose the hour, once again coronation ceremonies were held, and once again the king, with the name Shah Soleiman, placed the crown on his head and sat on the throne.

Chardin writes this story in great detail, expressing his astonishment regarding Iranians engaging in such futile efforts. According to what he wrote, and we also know from history, that action had no good result and had no effect on the affairs.

There is also another story that one of my acquaintances wrote about an astrologer. Here I will summarize what he wrote:

Three years ago, in the Islamic lunar month of Ramazan, a friend invited me to dinner to break fast with him. When I went there, entered through the door, and sat down, in addition to the host, there were two other people there. The host introduced them: "This gentleman is Mr. Mosavvar-Rahmani, who makes fine engravings. This other gentleman, Mr. So-and-So, is an astrologer. His astrology calendar is unique in Iran." He then introduced me to them.

The introductions opened the way to conversations. After speaking of this and that for a while, Mr. Astrologer turned to me and said: "I am astonished that you have not seen my calendars before. Don't you believe in latitudes and horoscopes? Don't you take into consideration good omens and bad omens in your affairs?"

The host did not leave me the chance to respond. He said: "Yes, now I remember that Mr. So-and-So is a supporter of *Peyman*, and he definitely does not believe in astrology."

The astrologer asked: "What is Peyman?"

The host responded: "It is a magazine that refutes astrology, divination, fortunetelling, and the like, and in its latest issue, it has published detailed articles about such matters."

The astrologer said: "That is nothing new. Every science has always had deniers from ancient times. Astrology has always been refuted by some group of people, and many books have been written to refute it."

The host said: "However, *Peyman* has something new to say. It writes: If it is true that an astrologer can have knowledge about the future, why does he not benefit from it in his own work?"

The astrologer asked: "What sort of benefit?"

The host said: "To buy certain goods that he knows will cost more in the future and sell them at a higher price, thereby making enough profit to not need to publish calendars and sell them for one rial. Moreover, the magazine says that if anyone could report about the future, governments could make the most important use of him and make him a millionaire."

Putting on strange airs, Mr. Astrologer said: "I benefit from all these things. You have no idea about my connections and the things I do. Just a few days ago, Mr. Jam (who was the prime minister at the time) sent for me, and when I went there, he asked me about the war of Germany against France and England and about when it will occur. He met me in private for two hours and asked me about these things. When the speaker of the parliament, Haji Mohtashemossaltaneh, wanted to go to Europe to attend the coronation of the British king, he sent for me, and when I went there, he asked about the direction of Mecca in London, so that his prayers would be performed properly. I am not supposed to tell you all the secrets. Every day, ministers send for me and ask me questions and I answer them."

As he was speaking, he was staring at us, apparently realizing that we did not accept the veracity of his words. That is why he suddenly changed his tune and said: "Would you like me to tell you a strange story?" And without waiting for an answer, he began speaking:

"The year when I went to Europe, in Paris, a professor came to visit me, because he had heard that I was an astrologer. He wanted to assess the level of my knowledge. He asked me a number of questions. I said: 'There is no need for all these questions. Think of a specific day and I will tell you what you had for lunch.' He was hesitant at first, but then he consented and mentioned a day. I described what he had for lunch on that day in detail. The professor was overjoyed and he took me in his airplane to various cities in Europe. Everywhere we went, he introduced me and referred to me as a great scientist."

Up to this point, I did not disrupt or interfere in what he said, but I could no longer tolerate the vulgar fabrication of lies by Mr. Astrologer. I said: "Let's change the subject."

Instead of being grateful, Mr. Astrologer asked why in a protesting tone.

I said: "Because all of what you said are lies."

He said: "Lies? Would you like me to prove them to you?"

I said: "I would like you to repeat the same thing that you said you did in France and tell me what I had for dinner last night. And in order to know whether what you say is the truth or a lie, here we have a telephone. These gentlemen can call my house and ask what I had for dinner last night."

He said: "Yes, of course."

Since we were at the table for breaking our fast, I decided to keep silent, but Mr. Astrologer continued his boastful claims, quoting stinging verses and Persian and Arabic phrases.

After the dinner table had been cleared, I said: "Now is the time for you to show your skills."

He said: "Amazing! Do you think it is that easy? To do this, I need at least three hours. And we cannot do it here." We all said that we were prepared to leave him in the room for three hours and wait for him in another room. He said: "Do you think I am stupid enough to let you test my scientific knowledge? It needs to be an official gathering, so that when you test me, I can receive a medal and have it reported in all the newspapers."

I said: "This is what you yourself suggested. Moreover, if you pass the test, the three of us will testify to it in newspapers and all the people will learn about it."

He said: "By no means! By no means! I would never do such a thing. You do not understand the value of science. I am the person who drew the map for all the streets in Qom. One day I went to Qom. I saw a European tourist who was looking at the minarets and wanted to know their height, but he did not know how to figure it out. Immediately, I measured their height based on the rule of the scale of the tangent and height parameter. The tourist was most astonished..."

He spoke boastfully and continuously in this manner for half an hour, praising himself. Even though we no longer bothered about him and already knew what we needed to know and would not lend an ear to his boastful utterances, still the astrologer would not give up. What was worse was that he used biting statements in Arabic, such as "the ignorant, not the knowledgeable, are the enemies." He also recited Persian verses, such as, "It is enough of a fault to be a man of knowledge and science."

I said to him: "If verses could accomplish anything, we have a great deal of them, such as, 'my brother's astrologer scared me crazy.' Or in Persian, 'may the tongue of the astrologer be ripped off.' What is the benefit of such words?"

Mr. Astrologer, however, would not let go, and in retaliation for the fact that we had not accepted his boastful statements, he wanted to start a fight. The situation became so tense that the host inevitably interrupted and silenced him, and we no longer stayed but left the gathering.

This is where the story ends. This is an example that proves that the capital for the business of such individuals is mostly shamelessness, impudence, and lies. Consider the lies this astrologer fabricated! These individuals lie a hundred times and still are not ashamed and do not stop claiming to know about the unseen. That astrologer is a greedy cleric who had accumulated great wealth through such deception, and every year he published an astrology calendar.

As I said, astrology is without foundation, as are telling fortunes and other soothsaying methods. For example, they say that such and such a star and another star have come together in such and such sign of the zodiac and that proves that such and such a king on earth will die.

First of all, we should respond that, to your eyes, those two stars seem close to each other in one place. In fact, they are thousands of miles away from each other. The sign of the zodiac that you mention is imagined. Indeed there are no signs of the zodiac or squares in the sky.

Moreover, what does the coming together of two or several stars in a constellation in the sky have to do with the dying of a king on earth? A king or anyone else dies when he is sick or killed by someone. These things cause death, which have nothing to do with stars.

Some of them who were Muslims have said: "We do not consider the motions of the stars and their positions to have an effect in the world, but God's will is that when stars in the sky are in a certain position, a certain incident will occur on earth."

I ask: "How do you know that? What proof do you have for such a statement? You state something that you have fabricated."

In any case, despite the fact that people in the past were enamored by astrologers, accepting what they said and if it turned out to be false, they justified and whitewashed it, because what they did was baseless, they were exposed and disgraced many times. There are many such stories throughout history. Here, I will recount one of them.

Similar to the Safavid kings, the Ottoman kings also adhered to astrologers. They retained them in their courts and made them their close associates. The chief astrologer, Hossein Effendi, during the time of Sultan Murad [IV] and Sultan Ibrahim, was a close associate of those two kings, who asked for his counsel in every affair. In this way, he accumulated a great deal of possessions and became wealthy. Still, an incident enhanced his reputation and status even more. When Sultan Ibrahim was killed, he said: "I knew this beforehand, and I had given warning." He showed his astrology calendar in which, along with his praise of the king, the lines were arranged in such a way that the first letter of each line was used to form words, and it read: "Death of Ibrahim." He said: "Since I was not allowed to write it openly, this is how I gave my warning."

From this incident, his reputation increased several fold and he gained high status in the government, and since after Sultan Ibrahim, his son succeeded him, the astrologer was also considered a close associate of that king. Two or three years later, some people found in his calendar, in his praise of Sultan Mehmed, the phrase "Death of Mehmed" and warned the king.

The fact was that the astrologer every year, in a different code that was known to no one other than himself, would predict the death of the king at the time in his calendar. If it turned out not to be true, it would remain concealed, and if it turned out to be true, he would reveal it and boast about it. The only thing was that that year, they figured out his secret code and exposed him.

When his secret was discovered, they drove him out of Istanbul and sent him to a village to live out the rest of his life.

However, the miserable man could not get himself accustomed to that life and keep silent. He wrote letters about his work. The chief cleric issued a decree to have him killed, and he sent someone to decapitate him. The person who would predict the death of others got himself killed in this manner.

4. Face Reading and Palm Reading
One method of soothsaying is face reading and another, palm reading. Face reading has been around for a

long time and is mentioned in Persian and Arabic books. Some individuals think that by looking at someone's face, they can tell about his future. For instance, they would say that that person has a wide forehead and will become wealthy. A person with connected eyebrows would become a scientist.

Palm reading, however, came from Europe and is a new thing. Some call it "European fortunetelling." Some people in Europe predict a person's future by assessing the lines on his palm, and they have devised guidelines for it. They have published books about it, some of which have been translated into Persian. Some people assume everything that comes from Europe is valuable and that is why they place great value on their fortunetelling and have brought it here for Iranians.

All of these things, however, are baseless. As I said, there is no method for knowing about the future. What occurs in the world has other causes which have nothing to do with the lines on one's palm or how this or that part of the face looks. For instance, a person's acquiring legitimate wealth depends on his efforts and then for events to also be compatible with his aspirations. A farmer becomes rich when he makes a great deal of effort in his work, plants a great deal of wheat, barley, and other crops, and then, when winter is not too cold so as to damage his cultivation, or when he has safety at the time of harvest so that the Lors or Shahsavan tribesmen would not plunder his harvest. It is in this way that he can become rich. How could these factors have anything to do with his forehead or the lines on his palm?

Even though palm reading came to Iran recently, we know about the harm it has caused. Two years ago, a young man was studying at the Police Academy. One of his classmates was a palm reader, who looked at his palm and said: "You will always be unfortunate and miserable." The inexperienced young man, who had many hopes for his future, including getting married to

the daughter of a rich man, upon hearing this prediction
suddenly was overwhelmed with despair and committed
suicide the next day. (Since his father is from Tabriz and
an acquaintance of mine, I learned about this story.)

As I have mentioned, there are numerous methods
of fortunetelling and soothsaying, and I will be unable to
mention and discuss each and every one of them. For
example, some people in Iran use the *divan* of poets for
fortunetelling. Some people use playing cards for this
purpose. Let me say it in a few words: All of these
things are baseless and engaging in them is nothing but
an indication of being addlebrained. We must make use
of our intelligence and wisdom and pursue paths that
result in living easier and more happily. We have no
need at all to know the future; rather, knowing the future, were it possible, would cause chaos in life. These
things are the work of those who cannot follow a straight
path and always follow a crooked path.

5. Divination

Divination is the method of fortunetelling of clerics.
Divination is used when someone wants to travel, buy a
house, or take a wife. He would go to a mullah, and with
his help ask God whether what he is about to do will turn
out to be good or bad. One of the functions of mullahs in
Iran is to perform divination. Large masses of the people
believe in divination. They think that it would be un-
godly not to consult with God in their affairs. However,
if you think clearly, you shall see that it is the same behavior as that of the idol worshippers of Greece toward
their gods and consulting with them in their affairs. (I
mentioned it in connection with the Delphi Temple.)

There are various ways of doing divination. The
best known methods are divination with prayer beads
and with the Koran. Since the practitioners consider
divination to be conversing with God and moreover they
need to speak in Arabic (such as, "I seek good tiding

from God"), hence, the person who performs the divination must be a mullah or a pseudo-mullah.

It is a spectacle when a man or a woman comes across a mullah on a street or in an alleyway and says: "Your Reverence, do a divination for me." The mullah immediately stops, puts his hand into his breast pocket, takes out a string of prayer beads, and then, mumbling a prayer, he closes his eyes, holds the prayer beads, fingers them, and says it is either a good or a bad undertaking, and then he starts walking away slowly and arrogantly.

Even more of a spectacle is the performing of divination with a Koran. Once the mullah opens a page randomly, he reads the verse and tells the person who has asked for divination, "My man of faith, the verse is about Paradise, it is a good undertaking" or "The verse is about punishment, it is a very bad undertaking."

Some of the mullahs have set up a more colorful business. The person who has asked for divination needs to write his question on a piece of paper, place it in an envelope with some money and seal it, and then send it to the mullah. In most cities, there are a couple of such businessmen, and people talk a great deal about the divinations they have performed and how they have turned out to be true.

As I mentioned, it is a way for the people to forget ten lies by a fortuneteller, astrologer, or divination businessman, but talk enthusiastically when one of their statements turns out to be true.

Thousands of people suffer damages from divination, but they try to justify it by saying: "It was in my interest to suffer this loss." But if someone somewhere undertook a venture and benefitted from it, they would make up exaggerated stories about it and say: "I believe in the divination performed by Reverend Such and So. I have experienced it myself."

Some people are crazy about divination, and they engage in it for everything they do. On the other hand, the mullahs consider it an obligation, and they think by divination, they are helping the people and facilitating their affairs. This itself is an indication of their childish minds and failure to understand God.

No one asks: Where did God make such a covenant with you to answer all your questions? When did He convey to you the mystery of speaking to you with prayer beads or through Koranic verses? Tell me, what is your answer?

And then, why do you not know that God has granted the people intellect and wisdom to discern between good and bad and profit and loss? Why do you not know that everyone must use his wisdom in his life? You who do not know these things, what right do you have to lead and guide the people?

One of our supporters has said it very well. He says: "God granted wisdom to human beings to discern what is good from what is bad. If divination with prayer beads were the way to understand the good and bad, He would not have granted wisdom to them, and instead, He would have created flesh prayer beads in their bodies, so that they would count the beads and discern good from evil whenever they needed to."

In any case, divination is worse than fortunetelling, because in divination they openly ascribe lies to God. Moreover, people do not believe in fortunetelling in the way they do in divination. That is why the harm of divination is greater than that of fortunetelling. If someone were to do research, he would find that thousands of totally harmful acts have taken place as a result of divination. Thousands of girls who have had good suitors have not gotten married because their fathers believed in divination. Thousands of good deeds have been disregarded because blind prayer beads have prevented them.

Chapter Two

Is There Any Benefit from Witchcraft?

As I mentioned, there are several categories of superstitions. The first category is about fortunetelling and knowledge of the unseen, which I discussed earlier. Another category concerns witchcraft and acts that deviate from the laws of the universe. As I mentioned, this world operates on the basis of a set of laws, and every undertaking has its own way. For instance, if someone is ill, if he wants to be cured, he needs to go to a physician and recover with medicine and treatment. A woman who seeks love from her husband and wants to live in tranquility and happiness needs to improve her own behavior, and if the husband is mistreating her, she needs to have some people to give him advice. A person who wants to become wealthy needs to choose a business path and work hard to acquire more money. These are the ways to do things.

Now we want to see, if one tries other ways that deviate from the ways mentioned, would he obtain results? Can an illness be cured by copying a prayer on a piece of paper and hanging it somewhere? Can a woman gain the love of her husband by burning a bone? Can one recite a prayer and get rich?

The answer to all of these questions is "no." We must say: "Outside the laws of nature, nothing can exist." Since various superstitious beliefs are also popular among the people in this connection, I shall discuss them one by one.

1. Witchcraft

In the language of the people, witchcraft consists of those evil things that practitioners of witchcraft do for women and others. What we have learned about the history of witchcraft is that in ancient times when there was little knowledge, since they did not know of any medicine or other treatment for diseases, everyone did what came to his mind. For instance, they would burn a bone and blow its smoke on the patient. They would circumambulate him or sometimes jump over him. They would feed him fetid water. They would do all sorts of similar things. Then appeared certain individuals who would visit ill people and with such superstitious practices, try to cure the patient. This was their profession. Then they expanded the field and used witchcraft not only for diseases but regarded it as effective in other affairs. Practitioners of witchcraft had high status among the savage masses.

Later, when sciences developed and medicine became more common, witchcraft did not disappear all at once. It survived here and there.

Then, at the dawn of Islam, a strange superstition appeared among Muslims, which was, since they considered Satan to have a hand in the affairs of the world, they figured that the effect of witchcraft was from Satan. They imagined that if anyone turned toward Satan and became subservient to him and did the forbidden acts that Satan wanted, Satan would teach him witchcraft and enable him to do anything he wants. Out of ignorance, they thought witchcraft was effective, and since they could not consider it as being from God, they thought it was from Satan.

This ignorant idea still remains among Muslims, especially women. They do not regard witchcraft to be from God, but they think it is effective. Practitioners of witchcraft tell such women: "If you want to achieve your purpose, you need to commit a religiously forbidden act."

This was a brief account of the history of witchcraft. The fact that it has been widespread is undoubtedly the result of the inability of the spirit and sluggishness of intellect. It is undoubtedly the result of egotism. Some woman experiences lack of love from her husband and instead of considering it the result of her own bad behavior or unattractive appearance and dress, because she cannot imagine herself to be bad or deficient, she considers it to be the result of witchcraft, suspects her husband's sister, her own co-wife, or the wife of her husband's brother, and thinks witchcraft is the remedy. Some man suffers from poverty, and since he cannot blame it on his own laziness or incompetence, he blames bad luck and seeks its remedy in prayer charms and a good omen talisman.

Whatever the case may be, witchcraft is one of the problems of the masses. Right here in Tehran, which is the capital of Iran, there are many practitioners of witchcraft who make a living by it, and some of them shamelessly have posted signs on their houses. These individuals are both fortunetellers and practitioners of witchcraft and try to deceive men and women by various means.

If someone were going to investigate, he would find that each of them is the cause of hundreds of evil deeds. Most likely, there are many husbands and wives between whom those individuals have created enmity and hostility. Most likely, those individuals have prevented many patients from going to physicians and have caused their deaths. Most likely, they have caused many chaste women to become unchaste. As I wrote earlier, there are many criminal files about the evil acts of these individuals in the Tehran Prosecutor's Office, which I will refrain from mentioning.

The thing which is more astonishing is that most of these practitioners of witchcraft are indigent hooligans, and it would be enough to say that their claims are baseless from the root. Why wouldn't a person who supposedly is able to move hearts by burning a bone, dying a sheep's head, or writing a talisman not benefit from his own talent? Why does he not try to gain the sympathy of the rich? Why does a person who can make others rich not become rich himself?

2. Catching Jinn

Practitioners of witchcraft engage in various types of deception. For example, they claim that there are creatures call jinn who, similar to human beings, live family by family, have their own kings, and live among the people. The difference is that they cannot be seen with the human eye. They say that if anyone harms them unknowingly—for instance, sprinkles water on one of their heads, or steps on them—that jinn will become his enemy, try to harm him by driving him mad, or afflict him with an illness. They say that such a person should go to a jinn catcher who would write a prayer charm for him or do some witchcraft for the jinn to leave him alone.

This superstition about the jinn has existed since ancient times, because they did not know the cause of some sudden diseases and considered them to be caused by harmful jinn. That is why insane people are referred to as stricken by jinn, which is a translation of the Arabic "majnun" (the Persian word is "div" which is the root of "divaneh," or insane). Among Iranians, there existed fantasy tales about "fairies."

Some practitioners of witchcraft claim that they dominate the jinn, that they can summon, command, and instruct any one of them they want, or that they can interrogate them and acquire information. If an item or money has been stolen, one solution is to bring a jinn catcher who will help catch the thief and the stolen goods.

I should say, all of these things are lies. The notion of jinn is fundamentally baseless. I ask, where are such creatures? What proof is there of their existence? And then, what are such creatures doing among the people? Are they there to be harmed and to become enemies? Suppose all of these ideas are true. Why does a jinn who has been harmed and has become an enemy not beat and kill that person rather than driving him insane? Can a jinn gain access to the human brain? After all this, why is the jinn afraid of some prayer charm or talisman? Why have such dreadful creatures become subservient to some hooligan? What part of all this is true?

I know that some people mention some verses from the Koran and consider them as proof of the existence of the jinn. That is why I respond and say: Those verses in the Koran are problematic and need to be addressed. In any case, we cannot shut our eyes to all that is known because of them. Under that pretext, we cannot accept the existence of jinn. I write once again that such creatures have not existed and do not exist.

Then, what does the existence of jinn have to do with the various claims of the jinn catchers? What proof is there for all this?

The books of the mullahs and Sufis also contain statements about the jinn. Some mullahs have claimed to be acquaintances of the jinn. Some have claimed to have taken jinn women as wives. Regarding the many followers of Sufis, they have written that some Sufis had jinn followers and that those Sufis would some days go among them and live with their devotees.

In Shi'ite books, the jinn are considered to be of two categories. Some have been considered to be Sunnis and some, Shi'ites. I am sure you have heard the enchanting legend of "Bi'r al-Alam" [The Well with a Flag], a story about Ali spending seven nights and days fighting with his sword to force the jinn to convert to Islam, and he made Asfar and his son Za'far the commanders of the jinn. You have also heard that on the day of Ashura, Za'far with an army of jinn came to help Ali's son, Hossein, but that imam did not consider the war between humans and jinn permissible and did not allow it.

Most interesting is the story of a mullah in Hamadan thirty or forty years ago who had said that he received news of the death of Za'far, and for this reason, he held a memorial service at his home.

3. Writing Prayer Charms

Writing prayer charms is another sort of witchcraft. This was created by mullahs so that they could do with prayers what the practitioners of witchcraft do with witchcraft, to cure the ill with prayers, to make the indigent rich, and to release the debtors from debt.

Initially, the mullahs began by writing prayers in their books about the curing of every illness or meeting every need, such prayers as "Omm Davud," "Omm al-Sabyan," "Jowshan-e Kabir," "Jowshan-e Saghir," "Harz-e Javad," and others, which are too numerous to mention. Many famous mullahs such as Seyyed ibn Tavus, Majlesi, Mola Mohsen Feyz, and others have written books in this connection. Later, prayer writers created a profession out of this, and since then, there have been one or several of them in every city.

Masses of women and men are most devoted to prayer writers. Those who would not visit a fortuneteller or a practitioner of witchcraft would not hesitate to visit a prayer writer. Worse than all this is that they imagine this practice to be attributable to religious belief and worshipping God. They say: "We want the cure for our ailments from God."

On the pulpit, the mullahs reprimand the people openly and say: "You have lost your belief in God. When you get sick, you go to a doctor. Why do you not get your cure from prayers?"

Observe the extent of ignorance! They do not know that God has shown a path for every undertaking, which must be followed. They do not know that God has made the curing of illness through remedies and taking medicine. Impudently, they want God to change His laws and behave as they wish.

Some people criticize me and say that I refute everything. My response is: My problem with you is reminiscent of the problem of the man who was in debt and when his creditor would come to his house, he would get angry and say: "You come and knock on the door of my house every day." The creditor replied: "Then what am I supposed to do? Do you want to not give me my money and for me not to come to your house every day?" I also say: "What am I supposed to do? Do you want to keep all your ignorant ideas in your brain and for me to shut my mouth and keep silent? Or do you want me to criticize you for one of your ideas and disregard another one? It is your fault for being so ignorant and misguided. That is why I criticize everything you do."

They say: "Then why is it that all those religious scholars have not figured it out?"

My response is: "You must ask them. Ask them why they have not figured it out."

The ignorance of the mullahs in this connection is not as simple as one might think. Their ignorance is clear proof of their being irreligious, because religion is for understanding God's laws and living accordingly. Indeed, religion is for the people to understand the world and life properly, and to find the proper way in everything they do. It is not for engaging in witchcraft and prayer charms instead of seeking treatment. Hence, citing and writing prayers instead of seeking treatment and considering it as cure is being irreligious, and the mullahs consider these things to be a part of religion.

The actual meaning of the statement of the mullah who says from the pulpit, "You have lost your belief in

God. When you get sick, you go to a doctor. Why do you not get your cure from prayers?" is: "This world and its laws are not from God. For medicine to cure illnesses and improve the conditions of the patients is not what God has set up." Does such superstitious belief not indicate lack of understanding of God and being irreligious?

Writing and reciting prayer charms, writing prayers to stop fever, writing talismans, and all such similar things are baseless and futile. In addition to being indicative of ignorance and misguidedness, they also inflict great harm. Many patients have set their hopes on these things, have not pursued treatment and medicine, and have said farewell to life. It has often happened that some ignorant people have set their hopes on prayers, have refused to engage in a profession, and have suffered a great deal of misfortune.

Moreover, one of the causes of the laziness of Easterners in making a living has been due to such baseless hopes and wishful thinking. Leaving the ordinary people aside, even kings and leaders have suffered and are suffering from such ignorance.

Most astonishing are the lies they have told and continue to tell. If there is a conversation in a gathering, they tell stories about the effect of some prayer and its proven results. Some reputable people would not refrain from fabricating lies in this connection. Emir Abdur Rahman, the famous king of Afghanistan, in his published writing tells a strange story. A sheikh had given him a written prayer that would protect him from bullets if he carried it with him. Emir Abdur Rahman says: To test it, I tied it to the neck of a sheep and shot a bullet at it, which worked.

See what a great lie a famous king fabricates! If such a prayer existed, Emir Abdur Rahman could have driven away the British from India with merely an army of a thousand soldiers and established a very great kingdom by giving each soldier a copy of that prayer to carry and be immune to bullets, so that whatever the enemy fired at the soldier would hit the ground and whatever they shot would bring the enemy to its knees. If this story were true, why did Emir Abdur Rahman not try to benefit from it?

Besides, the sheikh who knew such a prayer could have become a great king. He could have conquered Asia, Europe, and America. He could have taken all the treasures of the world. Then, why was it that he did not and instead extended his hand in need to Emir Abdur Rahman?

This story shows one thing clearly. It shows that Emir Abdur Rahman, similar to many kings of Iran, India, and Afghanistan, was a superstitious man who associated with deceptive sheikhs and vagrant dervishes. It is questionable as to whether a king with such a mindset would have been able to have the wherewithal for protecting a country. Was all this not indicative of his weak mind and will?

We also know another such story in Iran about Fathali Shah and Haji Mirza Mohammad Akhbari. It is said that when Fathali Shah was at war against the Russians and the situation had turned out to be difficult for Iranians, Haji Mirza Mohammad Akhbari, one of the mullahs, assumed the task of going into seclusion and prayers for forty days, and by doing so, kill the Russian commander, General Pavel Tsitsianov [whom Iranians called Ispokhdor or Inspecteur], and bring his head to Tehran precisely after those forty days. And supposedly, he had accomplished it. This story is recounted with much embellishment in a Qajar era book of history, *Nasekhottavarikh*, as follows:

> "After this incident, the prominent trustees of the government requested of Haji Mirza Mohammad Akhbari that better still would be the killing of the Russian emperor. He responded, 'Kings and emperors cannot

> be harmed as easily. I will even be killed for
> the murder of Ispokhdor, who was a great
> commander and strong soul.'"

Undoubtedly, however, this story is not true in the manner about which it has been written. Without a doubt, they have added falsehoods to it. As I have stated before, even those who do not ordinarily tell lies do tell lies in such instances. The likes of Emir Abdur Rahman also fabricate myths. One can also conclude from this story that Fathali Shah was a superstitious man who instead of mobilizing an army and weapons had set his hopes on such beliefs.

Let me conclude this chapter by saying that we have very strong overall proof for the baselessness of such superstitious beliefs. A country which has had the likes of Haji Mohammad Akhbari, in which hundreds of Sufi pivots have come and gone, in which thousands of deputies to the Twelfth Imam, manifestations of God, special deputies of the Twelfth Imam, and the like have made a living through such titles, a country in which hundreds of domes over the shrines of imams and their offspring have been erected, a country in which hundreds of prayer books have been authored, that country today lives in such misery and abjectness, as we can see. This is the clearest evidence that none of them have been or will be the source of any benefit to it.

Chapter Three

Can Certain Things Be of Good Omen or Bad Omen?

Another category of superstitious beliefs consists of regarding certain things as being of good omen or bad omen, which in Persian are called "marva" and "morghova." "Marva" means regarding something as a good omen and being happy and overjoyed about it, and "morghova" is its opposite.

Such superstitious beliefs are also quite widespread among the people and cause many problems.

Some days of the week are considered good omens, on which one can engage in any affair and be successful, and some days are bad omens, on which days one should not start anything.

Among the Islamic lunar calendar months, Safar is of bad omen, during which one should not have a wedding or similar engagements.

Among numbers, thirteen is a bad omen, and on the thirteenth day after Persian New Year, one must leave the city and keep the bad omens away. The thirteenth of Safar is a doubly bad omen. On that day, one should not engage in any undertaking whatsoever. Prior to the Persian Constitutional Revolution, on the thirteenth of Safar, all the bazaars were closed.

Among the birds, owls are a bad omen. Wherever they perch, death will occur. On the other hand, magpies are a good omen and a harbinger of good news.

Among animals, rabbits are a bad omen. If a person is traveling and sees a rabbit, he will not have a good time on that trip. But wolves are a good omen, and if a traveler sees a wolf, he will have a good time on that journey.

If a person sneezes when he is about to leave his house, it indicates that the outcome will not be good. He needs to forget about leaving or engaging in any affair, or wait a little before doing so.

Some newborns are good omens and some are bad omens.

Some brides bring good omens to their husband's home and some bring bad omens.

A tree that blossoms in autumn could cause good or bad omens. To prevent a bad omen, a sheep must be slaughtered.

A hen that crows like a rooster is of bad omen. It must be delivered to the house of a Seyyed, a descendent of the Prophet.

Some people have the evil eye and can harm anyone they look at. To prevent such harm, one needs to wear a string of glass beads or carry an "Ann Yakad" prayer charm.

There are too many such superstitions to be counted. Old women and old men are often the source of knowledge for such superstitious beliefs, and others can benefit from their very "existence." Every household has a Kolsum Naneh, or Aunt Agha.[1]

In the case of good omens and bad omens as well, there are many stories, and God only knows what harm such superstitious beliefs cause. Here I will write about only one such story.

In August 1941, the Russian and British forces invaded the Iranian borders, which caused chaos and lack

---

[1] Common names referring to old women who provide advice regarding such superstitions. [Translator's note.]

of safety throughout Iran. At that time, I had to travel to Borazjan. There are many sad stories about that trip which I do not need to write about here. I will write only about this story. In Shiraz, when we had gotten on a bus with a few people from Shiraz and Bushehr and we had heard some frightening information about the road ahead, a teacher was with us who was going to Gonaveh to open up an elementary school. He turned toward the other travelers and said: "Recite the *Qul Huwa Allahu* prayer six times and blow your breath in six directions. You can be sure that even if they pour bombs from the sky, you will be safe."

The travelers did as he had said. En route, they continuously shouted salutations to the Prophet and his family. Occasionally, as is common among Shi'ites, they also shouted some curses. The bus was struggling on the road and would occasionally stop in front of a roadside teahouse. What troubled me greatly was that after it had stopped and was about to start again, someone would sneeze. Everyone would shout: "We have to wait." The bus driver, who was even more superstitious than the travelers, would immediately stop. We would have to wait for a while longer, hear the shouting of salutations, and then, if no one sneezed, start going.

We stopped at a mountain pass in front of a teahouse. When we were about to leave, someone sneezed. I said: "Night is about to fall. We need to get through this nest of highway robbers as soon as we can."

They said: "Should we not heed the sneeze and wait?"

I said: "Wait for what? It is just sneezing. What does it have to do with our leaving or staying?"

Everyone was offended by what I said. The elementary school teacher began arguing and in a reprimanding tone said: "It is true that you have studied in Europe and are civilized. We are religious people and must behave in accordance with our religion."

I said: "I did not study in Europe, and what you are doing is devoid of religion."

After a long debate, the bus started on its way and night fell. We traveled for an hour, more or less. Somewhere on the road, we saw a truck that was stopped ahead of us, because rocks had been arranged to block it from moving forward.

When people saw the rocks, their faces drained of blood, because the arrangement of the rocks in that manner was indicative of highway robbers. They would block the road with rocks to force the vehicles to stop and they would attack and do what they did. We all knew there were highway robbers nearby. But the driver of the truck stepped out, removed the rocks, got in the truck, and began to drive. Our bus also followed him.

It was thought that there were no robbers, but half an hour later, when we arrived in Kazerun, we met and conversed with the truck driver and learned that what had happened was as follows: When that vehicle had reached the rocks and had stopped, suddenly three robbers with rifles had jumped out from behind the trees, had forced the driver and a woman who had been with him out of the vehicle, had stripped and robbed the driver of his clothes and money, and had robbed the woman of her suitcase full of clothes and her money, had ordered the driver to wait for half an hour and then to leave. The driver had waited for half an hour, and when he was about to leave, we had arrived.

After hearing that story, my fellow travelers were initially happy, since our bus had arrived later when the robbers had already left. Then, remembering the sneeze and the argument at the mountain pass, they all turned to me and in a victorious tone said: "Now you see, sir! Waiting after someone sneezes is the right thing to do. If we had not waited, wouldn't we have come across the robbers?"

Since they made a lot of noise, I said: "Keep your voices down. Just one of you speak and I will respond." They agreed and kept silent.

I turned to the school teacher and said: "In your opinion, is the sneezing caused by God, and does it mean that you should stop and not go?"

He said: "That was obviously proven. God wanted to protect us and that is the reason for the sneezing that occurred."

I said: "Then, why did God not want to protect the truck driver and that woman? Why did He not cause them to sneeze? Aren't they also creatures of God?"

Someone in the corner said: "Find out what sin they committed that God had them get in trouble."

I said: "They are just like you. Whatever sin you have committed, they have also done the same. Besides, does God get everyone who commits a sin into trouble? Then why does He not do the same to the robbers? Why did He not do it to Genghis Khan, Tamerlane, and Samad Khan? What proof do you have for what you say? When did God inform you that when you sneeze, you should stop and not leave?"

One of them said: "Didn't our Prophet report it?"

I said: "Where did he report it?"

After all the argument, the bus driver raised his voice and said: "I pay no attention to all these things you say. I have been a bus driver for fourteen years, and my experience is that whenever someone sneezes, I must stop."

After what he said, everyone got up and went about his business.

This was a sample of how the minds of Iranians have been contaminated with the superstition of bad omen. As I said, a series of these superstitious beliefs were the creation of astrologists. They assume that a proper hour must be chosen for every undertaking, otherwise it would not end well. On such a day when the

"Mansion of the Moon confronts Scorpio," one should not engage in any affair. Some other time, there is an eclipse and everything must be avoided. Such and such a day is in an ominous quadrature. Another time, "the Sun is in Aquarius." Such things the foundation for which is nothing but superstition are meaningful to them. Stars also are good and bad omens. The Sun is the "Grand Auspicious One." Saturn is the "Grand Ominous One." When a baby is born, based on the position of the Sun and the position of other stars at the time of his birth, they fabricate a "horoscope" for him or her. His good or bad life is dependent on that horoscope. There is so much of this that it would require lengthy discussions.

In past times when kings and prominent people retained astrologers in their courts and homes, an hour needed to be chosen for every affair. Often the coronation of a king would be delayed for weeks and months so that the auspicious hour chosen by the astrologer would arrive. (I wrote about the coronation of Shah Soleiman earlier.) The people have believed in such superstitions to the extent that we see them mentioned frequently in books, and often they have considered the inauspiciousness of the hour to be the cause. Ottoman books of history are filled with such accounts.

In our own time as well, while the astrologers have been disgraced and have no place in royal courts, their ideas have not completely lost their value. Today as well, if a king wants to be crowned, if someone wants to travel, or if a woman is going to get married, they choose the hour from an astrology calendar. Once again we see talk about "eclipse," "Mansion of the Moon in Scorpio," and the like. One of the functions of the neighborhood mullahs for the people is to choose the good hours on an astrology calendar for weddings, for traveling, for purchasing a house, and so on.

I must say that all these superstitious beliefs—both those that have existed and continue to exist among the people and those created by astrologers—are baseless. I must say that none of these good omens and bad omens are true. What is a bad omen and causes misfortune is being contaminated by such superstitious beliefs.

The days of the week are all the same. If you deliberate carefully, you shall see that the week itself is nothing but a figment of the imagination. In the operation of the universe, we do not see a seven-day cycle. In any case, Saturday, Sunday, Friday, and the like are names given to them and cannot have the slightest effect on the nature of those days.

The same is also true of the months, whether the Islamic lunar months of Prohibited Moharram or Blessed Ramazan or the Persian months of Farvardin and Ordibehesht. They are just names.

Regarding numbers, what is the difference between thirteen and twelve or fourteen? How did thirteen become a bad omen?

Owls do not and cannot cause the slightest harm to humans. Owls, magpies, and all other birds fly around for their food. They neither bring good news to humans nor inform them about death.

Rabbits are harmless animals that look for nothing but their food, and in any case, they are much better than wolves.

Sneezing, coughing, and the like are all functions of the human body and have nothing and cannot have anything to do with God's operation of the world. As I said about divination, God has granted wisdom, not sneezing and coughing, to humans to distinguish between good and bad.

A newborn baby and a new bride cannot cause good or bad fortune in anyone's affairs. This sinister superstition, however, causes hostility and can cause great harm.

All of these things, every one of them, are the result of ignorance. Because the people have not understood the causes and sources of the affairs, they have set their hopes on these superstitions, and since no one has tried to prevent them, they have established roots in this way.

People have firmer beliefs in the superstitions created by astrologers. Because it is called a science and is based on books, they are less suspicious. I must say, however, that these things are all baseless beliefs based upon baseless beliefs.

Neither are there any scorpions in the sky nor is the moon in anything. The twelve signs of the zodiac are given names. The explanation for them is that that endless space is seen as an azure ceiling on which the stars appear to be nailed. Since the moon, the sun, and the stars rotate and are in different places among the stars, in order to show their positions, ancient astronomers envisioned a belt-like shape in the middle of that azure ceiling (or as people call it, the sky) and divided it into twelve sections, giving each a name, such as Lamp [Aries], Bull [Taurus], Lion [Leo], Scorpion [Scorpio], Water-Carrier [Aquarius], and the like.

When they say "the Moon is in Scorpio," it is for showing the position of the moon; that is, as I have said, there is no scorpion in the sky. That sign of the zodiac is imaginary, and the moon is thousands of miles away from it. That is to say, what effect can the position of the moon in some sign of the zodiac have on the affairs of the world? Why shouldn't we engage in a certain task at that time? Can this be anything but bullying and shamelessness?

The Persian polymath Nasir al-Din Tusi committed an astonishingly shameless act in this connection, which must be remembered, similar to his other ignoble acts. This man did not personally believe in astrology, and for that reason, when the Mongol ruler Hulagu had set out from Hamadan to invade Baghdad and an astrologer under various pretexts was trying to stop Hulagu from going to Baghdad, Nasir al-Din began to speak to Hulagu, stated his reasons for regarding astrology as baseless, and urged Hulagu to go to Baghdad. Nevertheless, he has written a book on astrology and composed poetry, such as the following verse, about it.

> If the bathhouse is where you wish to be
> The Moon in the House of Mars must be

Whether to show off, or to misguide the people, he has written a book about something in which he did not believe.

Chapter Four

Can One See the Future in Dreams?

Another entanglement of the people is in connection with dreaming. Masses of people think that what they see in a dream is indicative of things which will occur in wakefulness. For instance, if someone dreams that he has lost a tooth, it indicates that one of his relatives will die. If someone dreams that he is flying, it indicates that he will be traveling or achieve high status.

It appears that human beings have believed in such things about dreams since the beginning, and that is why we find many such stories in the Torah and other ancient books in this connection.

We should understand, however, that dreams or signs that appear to humans after falling asleep are mostly the continuation of thoughts prior to going to sleep. It often happens that someone hears a story earlier in the evening, or has thought about something, and he then sees the same thing in his dream. Someone who has been contemplating a difficult issue and is pursuing it in his mind, should he fall asleep in that condition, is most likely to pursue the same issue in his dream, and it is also most likely that he will come to the right conclusion. I have experienced this many times myself.

Occasionally, dreams are things that one has heard or seen and he is unable to remember them while awake, but they appear to him in dreams. It is most likely that several different things are mingled and appear in an astonishing form. If one has experienced great fear or sorrow, his dreams will also become more disturbing.

A series of dreams are the result of human bodily desires and sensations. Men who desire women frequently see women in their dreams. A person who is angry at someone often fights that person in his dreams.

Most dreams are of this sort, although if science supports it, we would not find it farfetched to agree that some people would have dreams that come true. We would not find it farfetched that for humans (or some of them) there would be a hidden force for perceiving imminent occurrences, and for that force to function occasionally in dreams.

The only thing is that such dreams (if they exist) are one percent, or even one-tenth of a percent. When dreams can be either true or false, how can we rely on them? Suppose someone has dreamed that one of his relatives has come back from traveling. Can one say without a doubt that his dream is true and that relative will come back? Is it not true that one needs to investigate to see whether or not the relative returns and then know whether or not the dream was true? Could such a thing be worth the effort? How can a wise person set his hopes on that?

These are the things we know about dreams. We do not know how dreams occur. We do not know that what goes to sleep is the human soul or psyche. Science must clarify these mysteries. We know that one cannot place any value on dreams and cannot have faith in them.

However, as I said, masses of the people value dreams and recount every dream they have had that night during the daytime so that they themselves or someone else will "interpret" them and find some meaning. Many such people fabricate dreams and interpret them in an act of egotism and arrogance by saying: "My dreams turn out to be true. I have a pure heart." We have frequently heard such claims from corrupt and evil persons.

Women place more value on dreams than others. Here, as well, if they have one hundred dreams that turn out to be false, when one dream turns out to be true, or they thought it was true, they use it as a pretext and claim it as proof.

Many people also have distraught dreams about matters of no value which they embellish with lies to create something orderly and logical.

No matter what happens, some people say: "I knew this was going to happen. I had a dream about it."

If in a gathering someone talks about his dream, others feel the desire to fabricate dreams and recount them, each trying to make his dream more astonishing and worthwhile.

Altogether, dreams are one of the issues that trigger a sensitive weak vein in humans. This is the story of dreams. The more egotistical and feeble in intellect, the more the person is interested in dreaming and recounting dreams.

Some believe that the dead come into their dreams and speak to them, and that whatever the dead say is true. Many mullahs claim to have seen the imams in their dreams and asked questions of them. They claim that since Satan cannot follow the ways of the imams, those dreams are undoubtedly true, and they have undoubtedly met the imams.

I must say that all these things are baseless. That which appears in dreams stems from the human imagination. Outside that, there is nothing, neither imam nor Satan.

As I said, a wise man should not put any value on his dream, but should disregard it. During the day, he should forget what he dreamed at night, and if he remembers a dream clearly, and senses some meaning in it, he must keep it to himself, so that it would not become a pretext for those who engage in exaggeration.

Dream interpretation is itself another category of problems regarding which many books have been written, all of which are baseless. Since dreams are baseless, interpreting them is doubly baseless. Where does this idea come from that if someone dreams of something such as a horse, a camel, a bathhouse, grapes, or the like, or sees a certain happening in a dream, things like traveling, acquiring money, becoming happy, and so forth would occur? What is the connection between these things?

If you look at books written about the interpretation of dreams, you shall see that there is no logical reason except exaggeration (or better stated, bullying).

Sometimes people claim that they have tested the truth of those interpretations, but they are lying. One day someone said: "I have tested it. Whenever I dream that I am flying, I go on a trip." Another said: "I have frequently dreamed that I fly, but never went on a trip."

Here as well, one cannot believe these people. This is also an instance of occasions when even those who usually tell the truth lie. Many people also engage in self-deception.

Belief in dreams can also cause many harms. Those who believe in them sometimes become sorrowful and sometimes happy for no reason. At times they are hopeful for no reason, and sometimes fearful for no reason. Because of a distraught dream, they become suspicious of someone or other.

In my early youth, I had a friend. Rarely, did I find him to be in a normal state of mind. One day he would be overjoyed, and the next day he would appear to be sad. Once again, he would be sorrowful on another day. I asked him why.

He said: "Whenever I dream of black grapes at night, I get depressed the next day. I dreamed of black grapes last night, and I am depressed today."

I said: "What relationship could possibly exist between the black grapes about which you dreamed last night and your sadness today? What science would verify this?"

He said: "I have tested it, and you can see that because I dreamed of black grapes last night, I am depressed today."

I was astonished by what he said and felt sorry for his ignorance. I said: "If you think about it rationally, you shall see that your depression is the result of your false supposition rather than the result of the dream or black grapes. Because of such a supposition, whenever you have such a dream (and undoubtedly you have it often), you become depressed. If you discard that supposition, you shall see that neither are the dreams nor black grapes to blame, and you will not get depressed."

There is a verse someone has composed:

> If you dream of hens and fish
> For sure you'll be a king, if you wish

Thousands of people have been deceived by this verse. Since they had dreamed of hens and fish, they expected to become kings and set their baseless strange hopes on a bright future, often failing in their daily affairs.

Chapter Five

Can One Converse With the Dead?

Another superstition with which many are entangled is conversing with the dead. This superstition began in Europe and is something novel. Once, *kohen*s boasted of conversing with gods. Then came a time when jinn-catchers spoke with the jinn and fairies. Now, in the age of science, worshippers of superstitions have opened a new door and they converse with the souls of the dead.

We do not know when and how this superstition appeared in Europe. We do know that thirty or forty years ago, a large organization was formed regarding this issue and hundreds of thousands of men and women joined it. They published monthly journals, daily newspapers, and books about it. Hundreds of university professors supported it. Societies were established for this purpose. Thousands of men and women made a living by it. There were groups of spiritualists (*spirite*) in many countries.

This occurred in the West. In the East, however, the Egyptians were the first to acquire the idea and tried to spread it with astonishing enthusiasm. Monthly journals in Egypt, including *Al-Muqtataf* and *Al-Hilal*, contained many articles, and many books were published in this connection. Astonishingly, since they convinced everyone regarding the veracity of the idea and no one surmised its baselessness, some of the mullahs also regarded it as proof of the immortality of the soul and wrote about it in their books.

Later, the popularity of this superstition reached Eastern countries and some group in Iran also began to follow it. A group emerged in Tehran and they established a society. They held meetings in which they displayed their skills. Books were also written or translated in this connection, which they published.

As I mentioned, this is also nothing more than a superstition. Despite all the commotion in Europe and the United States in this regard and despite all those books published and the articles in newspapers, it is nothing but a baseless show.

I should point out that "table-turning" is the only thing which is accurate in this connection. Three or more individuals sit around a round table (which is placed on an iron bar and can easily turn). These individuals must place both hands on the table, all wish for the coming of a spirit, and concentrate fully. Once they concentrate in that manner for one or two minutes, suddenly the table is supposed to move slightly. This movement, in their imagination, is caused by the spirit who has come to converse with them. They say that the spirit uses their energy as a tool to turn the table. They match the numbers with a letter of the alphabet and learn what the spirit wants. This is the method of conversing. They assume that the spirits know about the future and the unseen and can answer any question they are asked.

This is all there is and one can observe in their meetings. This means that the spirits are in this world and can communicate with the living. That is why we should ask: "If this is true, then why do the spirits not turn the table by themselves? Instead of using the energy around the table, why do they not use the table itself as the tool? Then why is it that around their table should not be fewer than three individuals and cannot be one or two persons (unless they are very athletic)? Why is it that if one of the three does not believe and internally does not wish it, there will be no result? If a spirit indeed wants to show itself, it would be better with such an un-believing person who can be convinced to believe.

If they say that the movement is the result of con-centration and must be based on belief, my response is: "In that case, why would we need the spirit? Why not say that the show is the result of the efforts and concen-tration of the individuals, and that there is no spirit in-volved? What is so astonishing about that? When a per-son can be put to sleep and his energy taken with a glance (putting to sleep with magnetic force, or *magné-tisme*), what is astonishing about one or several individ-uals making a table move by concentration?"

If they ask, "Then where do those answers come from? At times information is revealed which none of the individuals around the table know. If a spirit is not involved, then where does the information come from?" my response is: "It has never happened and can never happen for an answer from the table with information that all three individuals do not know. The secret of it is that whatever every human being has seen, heard, or thought since childhood is accumulated in his brain, even though he does not know it and has completely for-gotten. These are the things that occasionally when one concentrates one remembers but imagines he did not know" (as is true in dreaming. The same mental reserves are shaken in sleep, mingle, and create strange things).

This is what others have said about this issue, and I agree with them. In any case, the only thing that cannot be agreed on is that the dead speak to the living and in-form them about the future.

If it were true that a dead person could speak, in cases of murder, why would we need to suffer and inves-tigate so much to identify the killer? Why do they not just summon the spirit of the murder victim and ask him or her about the killer? Instead of hiring all those inter-rogators and investigators in the Police Department, why not merely hire a few these spiritualists (or better stated, those who sit around the table)?

Leaving the governments aside, why in all the murders that occur where the killers are unknown does one of those spiritualists not step forward and display his skills?

If it were true that one could speak with the dead, we could discover many of the concealed mysteries of history. We could summon the spirits of historical figures to the table and ask then whatever we wished.

If it were true that the spirits know about the unseen and can inform us about the future, we could have thousands of benefits from that turning table.

This is indisputable proof that the movement of the table is due to the energy of those sitting around it. There is no spirit involved. More astonishing is that the spiritualists themselves, both in Europe and Iran, have not stopped at this point and have engaged in greater exaggeration and more lies. Some claim that they put a person to sleep by magnetic force, or *magnétisme*, and the sleeper communicates with spirits and asks them anything he wants.

Some of them say that the spirits speak to them and reveal themselves. Their books are filled with long stories about spirits coming to some spiritualist society when they were having lunch and playing music. There are stories about the spirits harming some family that was their enemy. The same stories which were told in the past about the jinn are now repeated regarding spirits.

There was one of them in Tehran, who said: "In Tbilisi, we put a Russian girl to sleep, summoned the spirit of Ferdowsi, and she recited the poems of *Book of Kings* with a Khorasani accent." Another said: "Ishaq al-

Mawsili and Parvaneh[1] come to me every night and sing for me." There is a ridiculous story about the same man, which I will recount here.

One day, he was busy in an office with his bombastic lies, also claiming: "Whatever question you have to ask your dead relatives, write it down on a piece of paper and seal it in an envelope. I will deliver it to the dead and get the answer written in his own handwriting."

An employee of that office, who was just as moronic and also a fabricator of lies, believed in what the man had boasted about, wrote a letter asking his dead father a number of questions, placed the paper in an envelope, and handed it to him. Weeks passed, but that boastful man did not show up. The man with the question sent for the boastful man, who eventually had to return. He tossed the envelope on the table.

The employee responded: "This envelope has been wrinkled and opened."

The boastful man said: "No, it has not been opened. Because the medium was angry, he crumpled up the envelope in his hand."

Then when he opened the envelope, he said: "But this is not my father's handwriting."

The other man responded: "We could not force your father to write it in his own hand. Someone else wrote it."

The employee said: "These answers are random. They have nothing to do with my questions."

At this point, since he could not come up with a response, he jokingly said: "Your father talked off the top of his head when he was alive. What can I do about his random answers?"

---

[1] Ishaq al-Mawsili was a singer one thousand years ago, and Parvaneh was a female singer who died over a decade ago in Tehran. The shameless bombast did not know any other name for fabricating his lies. [Note by Kasravi]

You can see that that addlebrained man had told a
lie and then had to cover it with several other lies. There
are many examples of this sort. I must say: "These people, similar to Shi'ites and Sufis, do not consider lying to
be a sin, and they are oblivious to being disgraced by
lying."

In a book published in Persian, they tell a story
about summoning the spirit of Hafez, the composer of
nonsensical poetry from Shiraz, and made him talk. The
spirit of Hafez supposedly told them that he was a contemporary of Sa'di. Whereas we know that Sa'di lived a
hundred years before Hafez, and those two never met.

Worst of all they say that spirits have not left this
world and each of them comes back to this world in the
body of another person. One of them in Tehran, who is
no more than a worthless idle babbler, claims that the
spirit of Mohammad ibn Abdullah (the founder of Islam)
is in his body. With this baseless superstition, he has
become emboldened enough to open his mouth and utter
such lies and ignorant statements.

Regarding conversing with the dead, this writer has
a personal story which clearly proves the baselessness of
the issue. For those who have read my *History of the
Persian Constitutional Revolution*, the name Asad Aqa
would be familiar. That young man displayed great
bravery in the Constitutional battles in Tabriz and became one of the famous leaders of that movement. Then
during the war of the people of Tabriz against Russia, he
displayed even more bravery, and later with other leaders of the fighters, he left Tabriz to go to Istanbul, where
they stayed for a few years and returned after the over-
throw and abdication of Nicholas II.

After Asad Aqa's return, we became friends and
socialized together for many years. Indeed, he was a
young man who was exemplary in everything. Alas, he
was killed in one of the battles of Simitqu [or Simko] in
Savojbolagh, where he was the commander of the gen-

darmerie. He became the victim of the evil intentions of foreigners and their accomplices.

At that time, I was in Mazandaran, and when I heard about his death, I became restless. The death of a brave young man would prevent me from sleeping at night, and I could rarely forget about it.

Years passed. One day in Tehran, once again I remembered that young man and his being killed. I wondered about what his old mother did. What happened? How could she bear the death of such a son? I surmised that she had also died and her soul joined the soul of her young son. I was reproachful of my brother for not writing anything about that young man's family.

This also passed. After a few months, one evening at the home of Sa'dodowleh, we had a gathering. I saw people sitting around a round turning-table, each deep in his own thoughts. The table occasionally turned and they spoke. I asked what was going on. They said that they were conversing with a spirit.

It was the first time that I had seen such a setup. I had seen many articles in the Egyptian monthlies *Al-Hilal* and *Al-Muqtataf*, but I had not read any of them. I only knew that many well-known scholars supported this form of summoning spirits and wrote books about it. That was why I had no ill suspicion about it and never thought it would be so baseless.

Hence, when once again they sat around the table and called me to join them, I agreed and went along with them. We were four people sitting around the table. We placed our hands on the table and concentrated. After a while, the table moved slightly and the conversation began:

"Who are you? A woman or a man? From which city?"

"I am a woman from Tabriz."

"Which one of these four people do you know?"

"Him (she mentions my name)."

"Which neighborhood of Tabriz are you from?"

"From Leylava."

My heart sank upon hearing the name Leylava, because the only woman I knew in that neighborhood was the old mother of that young man. I said to myself that my assuming that that woman had died was true. Like a thirsty person in the desert who has arrived at a body of water, I began asking questions. Whatever I asked, she answered by moving the table. All her answers were those I had assumed to be. In the end, I asked:

"Can you call your son to have a conversation with me?"

"I can."

"Then, let the sign be for the table to move."

After a few minutes, the table moved again and the questions began:

"Are you Asad Aqa?"

"Yes."

"What is the name of the city where you were last and in which you were killed?"

"Savojbolagh."

"How many years has it been since you went to the other world?"

"Ten years."

I asked question after question. I asked about his own condition. I asked about the late Khiabani. He answered all the questions. When we stood up from around the table, my whole body was shaking. It was as though I was in the same place with that young man and I was about to leave him. When I went home, I could not sleep until early in the morning. I constantly turned this way and that, struggling with various emotions and thoughts. Occasionally, I would say: "What a pity! There has existed such an easy way to communicate with the dead. Why had I not taken advantage of it thus far?" Then I thought: "Everything I asked, the answers were things I knew. I should have asked things I did not know." With such restlessness, I went through that night.

On the following day, I wrote a letter to my brother and asked: "When did the mother of Asad Aqa die? Why didn't you let me know?"

A week later, I received my brother's letter. He had written: "Asad Aqa's mother did not die for me to let you know."

The response shocked me. After thinking about it and evaluating it, I realized that all those questions and answers were from within me, and there was no spirit involved. This was when those baseless suppositions were uncovered, and I found how that table worked. Afterward, I went to Sa'dodowleh's home two or three more times, and once again tested it. All my testing resulted in the same outcome that there was no spirit involved, and that whatever it was had to do with those around the table. I thanked God for finding the truth so easily.

The astonishing thing was, how could something so baseless be supported by thousands of professors and scientists? Why were they writing those books? Why were they establishing those societies? From this, I realized how easily human beings can be misguided. I realized that science alone cannot prevent superstitious beliefs, and that if some superstitious beliefs are eradicated, they are replace with others.

As we saw, some of these people have used *magnétisme*, or hypnosis by magnetic force, to put someone to sleep as a tool for their deceptive work, and they pretend that when they put someone to sleep, he can communicate and converse with the spirits of the dead. They also pretend that the one put to sleep (or according to them, the "medium") with his own power or by conversing with the spirits of the dead can tell us about the future and the unseen. I should say, they have hundreds of ways for their bombastic talk and deceptive work.

We should know that this also is baseless. In this connection, the only thing that is true is hypnotism. That force exists in many people who can make someone unconscious with their glances, disable his energies, and make him a tool in their hands. The one who has been put to sleep is not conscious of anything, and whatever he does and says is by the instruction of the hypnotist. This is what it is. When they say they converse with the dead, foretell the future, and the like, these are all empty claims.

Chapter Six

Is the Control of Affairs Not in the Hands of Humans Themselves?

Another superstitious belief that we should consider among the worst is the superstition of luck, fate, and the like. Since ancient times, when people found someone to be successful in life and someone else not to be successful, and they did not know the cause, they imagined that some humans are lucky and some unlucky. This superstition appeared in the most ancient times and has spread among all masses of people.

Later, when religions and the understanding of God spread, the people considered all the affairs to have been arranged by God, and regarding the success or failure of humans, they created the superstition of fate, stating: "When God sends anyone to this world, everything that happens to that person is already inscribed on his forehead."

Then, when astrology became widespread, the astrologers colored that superstition a different hue. In their superstition, all the affairs of the world stem from planetary motions and the distance between the stars, and the success or failure of everyone in life is the result of his "horoscope" (the position of the stars at the time of his birth).

Then, in Islam, the idea of the "Preserved Tablet" emerged, and certain verses in the Koran which have not been clearly understood were used as evidence; thus, masses of Muslims ascribe all that happens to be due to the will of God and have considered human beings as having no will in their lives.

Altogether, a mixture of several types of old and new misguided thinking has spread a very harmful superstition among people, especially among Iranians and Muslims.

In this respect, it is a very rooted superstition, because it is expressed in various languages and under different names, such as luck, destiny, fate, lot, horoscope, and the like. On the one hand, it has been given the coloring of understanding of God and religion, and masses of people have thought that if they do not accept it, they have not understood God. Hundreds of hadiths and statements are written in books about this topic, such as the following examples in Arabic: "It will not occur other than what I will," "I recognize God through the revoking of determination and breaking decisions," "The lucky have been lucky in their mother's womb and the unlucky have been unlucky in their mother's womb," "Sustenance is divided."

On the other hand, this superstition has been a good tool in the hands of poets who live a life of abjectness and laziness in poverty and has opened vast grounds for their nonsensical compositions. That is why they have written in this connection and composed more absurd verses than any other:

> Yes, be it good or bad, fate is the harness
> And why all initiative shall go amiss
> No one can speak of the how or why
> Since the planner of such is beyond
>   how or why[1]

The myth of "sustenance is divided" is a good tool and pretext for a little poet who despite empty-

---

[1] These verses are by 12th Century Persian poet, Anvari.

handedness and panhandling claimed to equal the kings
and the powerful:

> For our poverty and frugality
> we are not ashamed
> Apprise the king that our daily bread
> is now proclaimed

The little man did not try to do any work, spent his
days in fabricating nonsense, and then, under some
pretext, he has stated:

> Should you even stitch the Earth to the sky
> It will not increase your daily bread supply

Sometimes they have pretended that not believing
in fate, destiny, luck, and lot means not understanding
God and not accepting His rules. One of them has stated:

> He had no understanding of God,
> nor of obedience
> Even luck and daily bread
> were mere expedience

Many of them have stepped further and pretended
that as the firmament revolves, all affairs are controlled
by it, and it is an enemy of the scientists and the good
people, since it always brings evil to them. That is why
they call it "a tyrant," "nurturer of the abject," and the
like. In this connection, they have gone to excess in their
ignorance and disgrace.

> The firmament grants the ignorant
> control of all they desire
> As a man of knowledge and virtue,
> you've all the blame you require

Sheikh Baha'i, who was a well-known mullah, is reputed to have composed the following two verses:

> Oh firmament, you help those
> who are ill-bred
> And constantly shower sorrow
> on the learned
>
> As you endlessly burden my heart
> with sorrowfulness
> You must deem me a learned man,
> that is my guess

One of the bad lessons of the "Tavern Dweller Poets," whose leaders were Khayyam and Hafez, is their excessive insistence on predestination. It provided them with a useful tool to say that "all that exists has existed and efforts have no result." Khayyam says:

> The sign of existence shall forever remain
> Using the pen for good and bad has
> naught to gain
>
> Fate has bequeathed you whate'er it deign
> Our worrying and efforts are in vain

Hafez says:

> Ne'er rely on action, oh Bard,
> as from the dawn of creation
> You know not what the pen of the Maker
> has written as your designation

This dark-hearted composer of nonsense has not neglected any myth in this connection. Occasionally, he has sought help from astrology and written:

> Grab the locks of a moon-faced beauty
> and do not feel sad

> Since from Venus and Saturn come omens,
>> be they good or bad

Occasionally, he delves into the myth of luck and says:

> From the dawn of time, the fate of dark destiny
> Cannot be washed white, this is a decree

Occasionally, he has pleaded with fate and has composed the following:

> I was forbidden to pass through
>> Good Reputation Gate
> If you do not like it,
>> change that fate

That Persian literature which they mention with their cheeks full of air and are proud of consists of such nonsense and misguided teaching.

Moreover, life itself has ripe grounds for the spreading of such beliefs and there are many causes for this. Since people are not aware of the world and the interconnection of affairs, inevitably, they regard events to be due to luck, fate, or stars in the sky, especially in instances when they collide with the inherent characteristic of "egotism." For some man who has failed to make progress in his life, it is difficult to recognize his own inability and incompetence and inevitably he blames it on bad luck and fate.

It is from here that abject and lazy individuals lean more on such superstitious beliefs. These are good pretexts for them not to deem themselves as failures in their abjectness and helplessness and not to blame themselves.

One could say that in the creation of superstitions, the human characteristic of egotism has been more effective than anything else. I have a story in this connection that I must write about.

If it has not been forgotten, up to thirty or forty years ago in Iran, people blamed every mishap on Satan. For instance, if two people began to fight, a person who wanted to mediate and calm them down would say: "Curse Satan! Recite the salutation to the Prophet and his family." The cursing and salutation were for the purpose of making Satan flee. Someone who had committed an evil act and would regret it would say: "May God curse Satan. Did you see what he did?" A person who committed theft and was caught, when he was interrogated, would express regret and say: "Satan deceived me."

This was a common practice in which ordinary people continue to engage. The educated, however, no longer believe in Satan and let go of him. The only thing is that the inherent human characteristic of egotism is still in effect. In other words, they have replaced Satan with other things.

For example, in Iran, where so much corruption and so many problems have appeared among the masses and caused their misfortune more than anything else, it is difficult for Iranians to shoulder the blame for their evil ways and to consider a solution for their corrupt behavior. It affronts their ego. That is why they blame everything on England and pull themselves aside.

No matter about what you complain, they respond: "It is because of the British. They are doing it, as you know!" With my own ears, I heard someone saying: "Majlesi[2] was motivated by the British to write those books and contaminate the people's minds with religious ignorance." According to an acquaintance: "The world's Satan is British policy."

---

[2] The reference is to Mohammad Baqer Majlesi, perhaps the most influential 17th century Shi'ite religious scholar.

I should not digress. These superstitious beliefs are also hollow and baseless. "Luck," "destiny," "horoscope," and such things are nothing but delusions. Human success or failure in life is nothing but the result of the competence or incompetence of the person and the favorability or lack of favorability of incidents.

Nevertheless, "fate," "destiny," or "predestination," which is a common belief among Muslims, are also all baseless. We can see clearly that God has granted people in this world freedom in their affairs. Everyone with his own free understanding and wisdom can engage in good and beneficial deeds or bad and harmful deeds. There is no compulsion.

It is true that humans are not in control of everything and we always face certain incidents in our affairs. For instance, a farmer can plant a tree in his orchard and benefit from it and can also not plant and not benefit, but the farmer who has planted the tree might not receive water and lose his tree, or his tree might be destroyed in a harsh winter, or some malcontent might yank up his tree and throw it away. Such an incident can happen in every undertaking.

The fact is that these incidents do not negate freedom. Everyone is also free to fight the incidents. That farmer can plant another tree and not lose what he wanted.

Another thing that must be kept in mind is misguided life and bad traditions. Today masses do not live by wisdom, and there is a dearth of judicious laws. That is why people suffer hardship and despite all their efforts have little happiness. Because they do not know the source of their hardship, they turn to believing in luck, karma, and the like.

One point that must be taught to the people is the very thing that humans can follow the path of wisdom in life, and that when they do not do so, they suffer. Hence, the suffering comes from them, not from bad luck, horoscope, fate, or destiny. In order not to have such suffering, instead of believing in superstitions, they must follow wisdom and find solutions for all problems.

Much has been written in books about fate and destiny, but all of it is hollow. The truth of it is what I have written here.

Sometimes those who use the "knowledge of God" as a pretext say: "Whatever you want exists and will exist. God knew it ahead of time. Hence, we cannot be free in what we do, because we must do what God knew."

My response is: "It is quite astonishing that you do not pay attention to what you clearly see, and you engage in something that is far away from you and you have no way of knowing it. You can clearly see that you have freedom of action. You can see that you are capable of anything. You disregard something which is so clear and talk about knowledge of God? I do not know what you have to do with the knowledge of God? From where have you acquired this understanding? What do you know about God to know anything about His knowledge? If you think that talking about God's knowledge is religion, I must say that you do not know the meaning of religion. These things are not religion, they are irreligion. It is irreligion when you do not engage in issues that have a clear path. It is irreligion that causes you not to think about the goodness of life and you do not use the instruction of wisdom, and make such excuses."

Khayyam, who was the leader of the tavern dwellers and always found excuses to express his hostility toward religion, has composed the following in this connection:

> From the dawn of creation, my
> drinking wine was known to God

Should I not drink wine, ignorance
is but this knowledge of God

You must tell him: "Since drinking wine is harmful, do not drink wine, and do not concern yourself with whether God knew or did not know. What you will be interrogated about is the drinking of harmful wine, and you will never be asked and taken to account about God's knowledge. And then, are you prepared to drink poison under the same pretext? Are you prepared to drink poison if it is placed before you under the pretext that God has known it from the beginning? There is no doubt that you are not prepared to drink it. There is no doubt that what you want is nothing but to make criticism and disturb the minds."

I gave a similar response to someone who one day said to me: "While you were traveling, I did not write a letter to you, so that I would receive a letter from you first. It is a bad omen to write a letter to a traveler right after he leaves."

I said: "What if the traveler owes you money? Would you not write a letter, but wait for him to write to you first? Is it not true that adherence to superstitions are only for when they are to your benefit, or it is compatible with your laziness and lethargy?" He laughed without responding.

This concludes my discussion, but I must say that whatever I wrote in this book, I have presented evidence for it. I did not consider it sufficient to say that there is no evidence for the veracity of these superstitions. I presented evidence regarding the falsehood of each. Altogether, I clarified the grounds, whether from the perspective of science, the perspective of religion and understanding God, or the perspective of benefits and harms to life. Nevertheless, I know well that, after reading this book, some people will say: "No, not all of the superstitions are false. Certain things are true." The secret to all this is that believing in superstitions has in most people become a sickness which will not leave them that easily. On the other hand, all of what I say consists of evidence that wise minds should accept. It would not be astonishing for those whose wisdom has been impaired to not be influenced by them. After all, I have no response to such people, and I know that they would not give up such superstitious beliefs and shall remain as they were.

This book is being published during the time when its author is hospitalized. Hence, for the followers or pure religion, this book is a memento of a sad historic incident.

Office of *Parcham*

Epilogue

Excerpts of M. A. Jazayery's article, "Kasravi, Iconoclastic Thinker of Twentieth-Century Iran"[1]

Ahmad Kasravi was born in 1890 in Tabriz, the seat of the Turkish-speaking northwestern province of Azer-baijan in Iran, in a middle-class family. He received a religious education in Tabriz, studied modern natural sciences on his own, and (as an adult) learned English at the American missionary school.

He was educated to become a Shi'i clergyman. However, he soon began to question the clergy's behav-ior—their hypocrisy, demagoguery, and greed; their abuse of religion; their obsession with the distant past and disinterest in contemporary problems; their disre-gard for the welfare of the flock; their divisive influence, which created and encouraged sectarianism; and, of most immediate concern, the violently hostile response of most of them to the Constitutional Revolution. His unor-thodox sermons and liberal activities, intensified after the Russian forces occupied Tabriz, added to his already well-known open-minded and liberal views on religion, attracted increasingly intense hostility from religious leaders. Mutual disillusionment was complete, and he

---

[1] For the full article, see Mohammad Ali Jazayery, "Kasravi, Iconoclastic Thinker of Twentieth-Century Iran," in Ahmad Kasravi, *On Islam & Shi'ism*, translated from the Persian by M. R. Ghanoonparvar, 2nd printing (Costa Mesa, CA: Mazda Publishers, 2019), pp. 1-53.

left the profession. He was off and on excommunicated by several other clergymen.

In the early 1930s, Kasravi began a new career as a social thinker. From then until his death, he studied Iran's social problems in detail, and suggested solutions for them. In broader terms, he also discussed Middle Eastern and world problems. In time, he developed a comprehensive ideology covering all aspects of society and culture. This was his central concern during this period, but he did not give up his scholarship. In fact, his major scholarly work, of more than 2400 pages (in the original edition), the history of the Constitutional Revolution, was written during these years, as were numerous articles on Persian grammar and on language reform, as well as other subjects.

Kasravi's ideology, and his approach to analyzing the social and political problems of Iran (and to offering solutions), was based on certain premises and principles. An understanding of some of these at the outset is important.

The most important premise, basic to all Kasravi's teachings, and one that he discussed repeatedly, is the primacy of ideas as determinants of human action: a person's ideas, beliefs, dictate his behavior. He often summarized this premise in the statement: "The source of man's ideas is his brain; and the brain is ruled by the ideas that are in it."

Another premise is that Iran's social ills (and political problems) are all interrelated. You cannot solve them separately. For example, you cannot successfully fight despotism without fighting religious superstitions, fatalism, certain parts of classical Persian poetry, and so on.

A third premise is that Iran's problems are not of recent origin. They are of long standing, accumulated during what he called Iran's "Dark Ages" (from the time of the Seljuq dynasty to the latter part of the Qajar period, approximately 1040-1850).

A major cause of factionalism in Iran is religious division. In addition, Kasravi found each religion containing objectionable teachings not conducive to democratic life. Since the religion of the majority of the Iranians, and the state religion, is Shi'ism, he spent a considerable amount of time in a detailed analysis and critique of that religion.

Kasravi's approach to Islam begins with two general assumptions. First, there are two Islams: True Islam, which was founded by Mohammad, and remained more or less in effect for several centuries; and what passes for Islam today, coming in many sects and forms. These two Islams have little of significance in common, and in some ways even contradict each other. The original Islam spread so far and so fast, and had such great success in the world, as a state and as a civilization. Today, on the other hand, Moslems all over the world are inferior in culture and subordinate to others. Secondly, even in its true form, Islam could not meet the needs of a much more complex world; nor should it be expected to.

Mohammad's Islam, broadly considered, had two components: the ideological and the political. The beliefs forming the ideological component have lost their force because of the development, among the Moslems, of certain ideas and philosophies, old and new.

As for Islam's political component, it has lost its relevance. Moslems long ago gave up the notion of a single Moslem "community," upon which Islam's political system was based. Moslems now live as separate nation-states. (Indeed, even Moslem Arabs, sharing a common language as well, now form several independent governments.) Islamic laws (*fiqb*) have been set aside, replaced with Western or Westernized laws. Any attempt to revive them could not succeed, since they would conflict with the intellectual, psychological, and general make-up of today's society.

Kasravi's opponents brought up several points, or "excuses" as he called them, in response to his observations. One was: "If the people are bad, how is that the fault of religion?" Kasravi's answer: "...The fault of religion is that it has lost its essence [*gowhar*]; that it has transformed into ten or more varieties; that it has changed from worshipping God to worshipping human beings; that it has come to be full of baseless superstitions and silly legends; that it has fallen away from the times and cannot guide the people; that it teaches its followers to pay no attention to life, and be pre-occupied with the dead; that it teaches people to be expecting some invisible man [i.e., the Hidden Imam]. What greater fault is there?"

Another response was: "People do not practice the religion. If they do, everything will be set right." He said: "It is far better that they do not practice it;" and gave examples of what might happen if they did: aggravated sectarian conflict, greater emphasis on pilgrimage to various tombs, and so on. "What, except harm, can result from practicing a series of irrational baseless acts?"

When Kasravi criticized some belief or practice common among the Moslems, some people would say, "This was not in the original [religion]." Kasravi's comment was: "What does the original religion have to do with you? You are nowhere near the original religion. *The religion of a people is that which they actually practice* [emphasis added]. Religion is not clothes, of which one may get two suits: one to wear, and the other to keep in the closet." He then asked Moslems how they would react if Christians, Jews, Zoroastrians and others took the same position; for, after all, those parts of their religions which are objectionable did not exist in their original religions.

Another concept, related to the "original Islam" argument, was expressed by his opponents in the sentence,

"We will return the religion to its original form" or "We will reform Islam." These ideas were not new, even in Kasravi's time. To begin with, he said, nobody has done anything but talk about doing these things. Secondly, he asked them if they knew what the original Islam was; and, if so, why had they abandoned it to begin with.

As was to be expected, in this debate about Islam, Kasravi's opponents often invoked the Koran. Thus, when he criticized some belief or practice among the Moslems, some people would say that the criticism was not valid. "Our book," they would say, "is the Koran. Are such practices in the Koran?" To answer this, he sometimes used an analogy: what they were saying was like the comment by a robber who, having been criticized for what he does, says: "These things [i.e., robbery, etc.] are not [permitted] in the Constitution. Our country's book is the Constitution. Does it permit robbery or banditry?" Kasravi then, referring to a certain practice among the Shi'ites, said: "Somebody should tell them: If it is not in the Koran, why do you do it? Somebody should tell them: It is not in the Koran, but it is in your traditions [*hadiths*]; it is in your *fiqh* books..."

Some said, "We will put the Koran in front of us, accepting whatever it says, and rejecting whatever it does not say." Kasravi said: "But have you not had the Koran in front of you all along? Furthermore, you seem to forget that all the various sects base themselves on the Koran, and none of them considers itself outside the Koran." Finally, Kasravi said that the Koran could not by itself solve problems, not even in Mohammad's time. Mohammad and his supporters had to do many other things, including taking armed action.

Kasravi questioned the Moselms' insistence that the contents of the Koran will forever remain valid. Thus, he reminded them, it permits slavery; it does not advocate democracy; it assumes the earth to be flat, and so on. He was equally critical of those who criticized the Koran on such grounds. Both groups were wrong because, he said, they were confused about the work of a prophet, and the purpose of the Koran. The essence of the Koran, he believed, is to be found in those verses which provide guidance in social behavior. It is in this area that a prophet's responsibility lies. On all other matters (science, history, etc.), he knows only what his contemporaries know.

Kasravi made an interesting observation about the Koran which is general, going beyond particular questions such as those mentioned above. It concerns the ability of the Koran to exert influence on the world of today: When it appeared in seventh-century Arabia, making such a great impact, there was no other book there to read. Today, people read many other books, and thus are subject to influences from many sources.

The Koran, in other words, has lost its effectiveness, and it is used by people for their own ends. Referring to those who insist they can find everything in the Koran, he said: "The Koran, in their hands, is 'the tree of a thousand-and-one fruits.' What they do with the Koran is like what is done by a man who has a tree in his house and pretends that it can bear any kind of fruit, and so he buys every fruit that is in season, ties it with a string to the tree, and shows it to the people."

SELECTED BIBLIOGRAPHY
OF THE WRITINGS OF AHMAD KASRAVI

Afsaran-e Ma [Our Officers]. Tehran: 1323 [1944/45].

A'in [Creed]. Tehran: 1311 [1932/33].

Az Sazman-e Melal-e Mottafeq Cheh Natijeh Tavanad Bud? [What Will Be the Result of the United Nations?]. Tehran: 1324 [1945/46].

Baha'igari [Baha'ism]. Tehran: 1322 [1943/44].

Bahmanmah-e 1323 [Bahman, 1323]. Tehran: np, nd.

Chand Tarikhcheh [Some Histories]. Tehran: 1314 [1935/36].

Dadgah [Court of Justice]. Tehran: 1323 [1944/45].

Dah Sal dar Adliyyeh [Ten Years in the Justice Department]. Tehran:np, nd.

Dar Pasokh-e Bad-Khahan [Response to Ill Wishers]. Tehran: np, nd.

Dar Piramun-e Adabiyyat [On Literature]. Tehran: 1323 [1944/45].

Dar Piramun-e Islam [On Islam]. Tehran: 1322 [1943/44].

Dar Piramun-e Falsafeh-ye Yunan [On Greek History]. Tehran: 1344[1965/66].

Dar Piramun-e Janevaran [On Animals]. Tehran: 1324 [1945/46].

Dar Piramun-e Kherad [On Rational Faculties]. Tehran: 1322[1943/44].

Dar Piramun-e Ravan [On the Soul]. Tehran: 1324 [1945/46].

Dar Piramun-e Roman [On Fiction]. Tehran: 1322 [1943/44].

Dar Piramun-e She'r va Sha'eri [On Poetry and Poetry Writing]. np,nd.

Dar Rah-e Siyasat [On the Path of Politics]. Tehran: 1324 [1945/46].

Din va Danesh [Religion and Science]. Tehran: 1319 [1940/41].

Din va Jahan [Religion and the World]. Tehran: 1323 [1944/45].

Dowlat be Ma Pasokh Dehad [Let the Government Respond to Us]. Tehran:1323 [1944/45].

Emruz Char-e Chist? [What Is the Cure Today?]. Tehran: 1324 [2945/46].

Emruz Cheh Bayad Kard? [What Must Be Done Today?]. Tehran: 1320 [1941/42].

Enkizisiyon dar Iran [Inquisition in Iran] (incomplete). Tehran: 1322 [1943/44].

Farhang Ast Ya Neyrang? [Is It Culture or Deception?]. Tehran: 1323:[1944/45].

Farhang Chist? [What Is Culture?]. Tehran: 1322 [1943/44].

Goft va Shenid [Conversation]. Tehran: 1323 [2944/45].

Hafez Cheh Miguyad? [What Does Hafez Say?]. Tehran: 1322 [1943/44].

Kafnameh [The Book of Kaf]. np, nd.

Kar va Pisheh va Pul [Work, Profession and Money]. Tehran: 1323 [1944/45].

Khaharan va Dokhtaran-e Ma [Our Sisters and Daughters]. Tehran: 1323[1944/45].

Khoda Ba Mast [God Is With Us]. Tehran.

Ma Cheh Mikhahim? [What Do We Want?]. Tehran: 1319 [1940/41].

Mardom-e Yahud [The Jewish People] (incomplete). Tehran: np, nd.

Mashrut-e Behtarin Shekl va Akherin Natijeh-ye Andisheha-ye Nezhad-e Adami Ast [Constitutionalism Is the Best Form and the Best Result of Human Thought]. np, nd.

Mosha'sha'iyan [The Mosha'sha'is]. Tehran: 1324 [1945/46].

Namha-ye Shahrha va Deyhha [The Names of Cities and Villages]. Tehran:1308 [1929/30].

Nik va Bad [Good and Evil]. Tehran: 1323 [1944/45].

Pendarha [Superstitions]. Tehran: 1322 [1943/44].

Peydayesh-e Amrika [The Creation of America]. Tehran: 1324 [1945/46].

Porsesh va Pasokh [Question and Answer]. Tehran: 1325 [1946/47].

Qanun-e Dadgari [The Law of Adjudication]. Tehran: 1312 [1933/34].

Rah-e Rastegari [Path to Salvation]. Tehran: 1316 [1937/38].

Sarnevesht-e Iran Cheh Khakhad Bud? [What Will Be the Fate of Iran?]. Tehran: 1324 [1945/46].

Shahriyaran-e Gomnam [The Unknown Monarchs]. Tehran: 1307-1309 [1928-31].

Sheykh Safi va Tabarash [Sheykh Safi and His Ancestry]. Tehran: 1323 [1944/45].

Shi'igari [Shi'ism]. Tehran: 1322 [1943/44].

Sizdahom-e Mordad [Thirteenth of Mordad]. Tehran: 1323 [1944/45].

Sufigari [Sufism]. Tehran: 1322 [1943/44].

Tarikhcheh-ye Chopoq va Ghalyan [The History of Clay Pipes and Water Pipes]. Tehran: 1323 [1944/45].

Tarikhcheh-ye Shir va Khorshid [The History of the "Lion and Sun"]. Tehran: 1309 [1930/31].

Tarikh-e Hijdah Soleh-ye Azarbayjan [The Eighteen-Year History of Azarbaijan]. Tehran: 1313-1319 [1934-41].

Tarikh-e Mashruteh-ye Iran [The History of the Iranian Constitutional Movement. Tehran: 1319-21 [1940-43].

Tarikh-e Nader Shah [The History of Nader Shah]. Tehran: np, nd.

Tarikh-e Pansad Saleh-ye Khuzestan [The Five-Hundred-Year History of Khuzestan. Tehran: 1312 [1933/34].

Varjavand Bonyad [Sacred Foundation]. Tehran: 1322 [1943/44].

Yekom-e Azar-e 1322 [The First of Azar, 1322]. Tehran: 1323 [1944/45].

Yekom-e Azar-e 1323 [The First of Azar, 1323]. Tehran: np, nd.

Yekom-e Deymah-e 1322 [The First of Dey, 1322]. Tehran: 1323 [1944/45].

Yekom-e Deymah-e 1323 [The First of Dey, 1323]. Tehran: np, nd.

Yekom-e Deymah va Dastanash [The First of Dey and It's Story]. np,nd.

Zaban-e Azari [The Azari Language]. Tehran: np, nd.

Zaban-e Farsi [The Persian Language]. Tehran: 1316 [1937/38].

Zaban-e Pak [Pure Language]. Tehran: 1322 [1943/44].

Zendegani-ye Man [My Life]. Tehran: 1323 [1944/45].

About the Translator

M. R. Ghanoonparvar is Professor Emeritus of Persian and Comparative Literature at The University of Texas at Austin. He is the recipient of the 2008 Lois Roth Prize for Literary Translation, a Lifetime Achievement Award from the American Association of Teachers of Persian, as well as a Lifetime Achievement Award from *Encyclopædia Iranica*. His recent books include *From Prophets of Doom to Chroniclers of Gloom* and *Iranian Cities in Persian Fiction*. His most recent translations include Shahrokh Meskub's, *Leaving, Staying, Returning*; Moniro Ravanipour's *The Drowned* and *These Crazy Nights*; Ghazaleh Alizadeh's *The Nights of Tehran* and *Two Views and Trial*; and Shahrnush Parsipur's *Blue Logos*. His forthcoming translations include Hossein Atashparvar's *From the Moon to the Well*, and Reza Julai's *Jujube Blossoms*.

<u>Books by Ahmad Kasravi Published by This Press</u>

On Islam & Shi`sm
Translated from the Persian by M. R. Ghanonparvar
Introduction by M. A. Jazayery
(1990, reprinted in 2019)

History of the Iranian Constitutional Revolution, Vol. I
Translated from the Persian by Evan Seigel
(2006)

History of the Iranian Constitutional Revolution, Vols. II & III
Based on a translation by Evan Seigel
(2015)

<u>Of Related Interest</u>

Sadeq Hedayat
The Myth of Creation
Translated from the Persian by M. R. Ghanoonparvar
Illustrated by Kaya Behkalam
(1998)

Hedayat on Religion
Edited by Paul Sprcahman and M. R Ghanoonparvar
(2024)

Ali Dashti
Twenty-Three Years
A Study of the Prophetic Career of Mohammad
Translated from the Persian by F. R. C. Bagley
(1994, 10th printing in 2021)